Illustration by Hiromu Arakawa

FULLMETAL ALCHEMIST

The Land of Sand

Volume 1
The Land of Sand

MAKOTO INOUE

Original Concept by
HIROMU ARAKAWA

Translated by
Alexander O. Smith
with Rich Amtower

VIZ Media
San Francisco

FULLMETAL ALCHEMIST vol. 1 THE LAND OF SAND
© 2003 Hiromu Arakawa, Makoto Inoue/SQUARE ENIX.
First published in Japan in 2003 by SQUARE ENIX CO., LTD.
English translation rights arranged with SQUARE ENIX CO.,
LTD. and VIZ Media, LLC.

Illustrations by Hiromu Arakawa
Cover design by Amy Martin
English translation © VIZ Media, LLC
All rights reserved.

Published by
VIZ Media, LLC
PO Box 77010
San Francisco, CA 94147

www.viz.com

Printed in Canada

First printing, September 2005
Second printing, October 2006

Contents

The Land of Sand

Bonus Story

Prologue

IT WAS A WASTELAND the color of yellow mud.

On a dry edge of it, a girl of seven, perhaps eight, lay flat upon the ground. Her eyes shone clear and bright above peach-colored lips, and her brown hair was bound in two pigtails that reached to her shoulders, framing a face that would be cute if only she were smiling.

But her cheeks trembled and her eyes glistened, betraying the tears she fought so hard to hold back.

An iron cart lay on its side, on her legs.

The girl whimpered.

She had been playing, drawing pictures on the ground with a stick. Like so many times before, she had run up and grabbed the cart, but this time, it toppled.

She looked up, longing to cry, but forcing herself to stay quiet. She tried to crawl out from under the cart, but only managed to scrape her arms. A sob caught in her throat, and she hiccupped.

It took all her strength to twist her upper body around far enough to see the houses on the outskirts of town, dim through the dust.

"Papa!" she cried out as loudly as she could. But she knew no one would hear her.

What would happen if no one found her, she wondered. What if she were stuck here forever? Fear gripped her and the dam broke. She wept, tears streaking the dust on her face, running grimy rivulets down her cheeks.

A shadow fell across her.

"Papa!"

"It's okay. I'll get you right out. Don't cry."

She blinked and looked up at the unexpected voice emanating from the dark silhouette of a boy framed by the sun. His face was hidden in shadow, but she could tell from his height and the sound of his voice that he was young, perhaps no older than she.

"Just hold on a second, okay?" He peered down at her. "Does it hurt?" he asked, giving the cart a light push.

It was all she could do to nod yes.

"There's an iron frame under the cart. See? That's what's trapped your leg. You'll be fine. It doesn't look like you're hurt."

Even empty, the iron cart was quite heavy. It was built tough for carrying heavy rocks. If the frame hadn't stopped it from falling directly on her, she might have been badly injured—unable to move or call for help at the very least.

"Hold on. I'll get it off you." The boy didn't seem intimidated by the cart's weight. He looked as though he might try to push it off her with brute force alone. As she watched, the boy took a step back. "Stay calm, and don't move."

He reached out with both hands and touched the frame under the side of the cart.

The girl barely had time to wonder what he was doing when she felt the weight of the cart ease. She looked down at her feet and saw the cart lurch upright and over. The iron bar on her legs had been knocked flat under the cart, but now it pointed straight up, as though it had sprung up from the ground like a plant . . . as though it was the bar itself that had leapt up and pushed aside the cart. Bewildered, she looked down to see the boy kneeling by her feet.

"Hmm . . . Looks like you got scratched up a bit, that's all. You're lucky!" The boy turned toward her and smiled, the sun shining on his face. It wasn't a face she recognized. He wasn't from town.

"Who are you?"

The boy brushed a shock of golden-blond hair out of his eyes and held out his hand. "Edward Elric. Nice to meet you!"

He smiled, his silver eyes sparkling in the sun.

Chapter One

Golden Hair

"You *sure* this is the right place?"

"Pretty sure . . ."

"It doesn't *look* like the right place."

"It doesn't, does it . . ."

The two boys hunched over the map spread out between them.

"This *has* to be it!"

"Well, the old geezer at the station said we'd find it at the end of these rails."

They looked down at the rails stretching out in a perfectly straight line from the toes of their boots. Straight. Not even a hint of a curve. There was no way they could have gotten lost.

"Across the carpet of green, to the mountains of hope, and the tall peak shining of gold," recited Edward, scanning the land ahead of them. "This sure doesn't look like Xenotime—like a town of gold."

"No, it doesn't," Alphonse agreed.

Edward Elric was dressed in black, save for a pair of white gloves and a red coat. A long braid of golden-blond hair hung down his back. His eyes were the same color as his hair, and they shone with a steely confidence and resolve. Though he seemed a bit cocky for his age, Edward carried the burden of a troubled past—one that had left him with a right hand and left leg of auto-mail.

His companion, Alphonse Elric, was his younger brother.

Alphonse was entirely encased in a suit of bronze-hued armor so large that it was hard to imagine the boy inside was a full year younger than Edward. And in truth, there was no boy inside. The suit of armor was empty. The only thing that made him a person instead of a heap of metal was a single letter written in blood on the inside of the armor that bound Alphonse's soul inside it.

In comparison to the giant suit of armor, Edward, who was already short for his age, looked even smaller, and few who saw him believed he was the elder of the two.

"We've been walking so long, I can't believe we haven't seen any people!" Edward turned and gazed at the rails stretched out behind them. He could see the station they had departed from, far off in the distance. Ahead of them, the rails continued on until they were swallowed up by the town. The entire time they had been walking, they had seen no one, nor had anything come down the tracks.

Xenotime, the Town of Gold. The two brothers were well versed in the legends of this town whose mountain had held extraordinarily rich veins of gold. Never at a loss for raw material, the town's goldsmiths were unparalleled, and Xenotime goldware sold for a premium price. Once a green agricultural town, Xenotime was said to be a paradise where gold glittered between every swaying blade of grass. The brothers knew the first gold rush was long gone and that they were arriving well past the town's peak. Still, they hoped for at least a glimpse of the glory that was Xenotime, land of plenty.

They saw nothing but a land of sand.

The rails that had led them there were coated with rust, and the wooden ties beneath were rotted and splintered. When the wind blew, the dust rose and hid the far-off houses beneath a haze. Beyond the town loomed a bizarre hulk that must once have been a great mountain. Cut to bits and dug out, it was a husk of its former self. All that remained was countless piles of rock like stacks of firewood.

Abandoned mining carts, rocks, and sandy gravel—barely contained by rusted iron fences—lay by the tracks. It was a desolate scene.

A small iron crane was set into the brown earth nearby. A lone pulley on a chain hung from it, rattling in the wind.

"Looks like none of this has been used in a long time." Edward pointed at the crane, red with rust. "This tower looks like it would fall over if you poked it with your finger."

Edward laughed and leaned on one of the rusty supports. The crane lurched to the side.

"Yikes!"

He hadn't meant to knock the crane over, and now it was too late to stop it. It collapsed with a long, weary shriek of metal. Edward was speechless.

"Looks like you're right, Ed."

Edward stared at the crane sprawled on the ground. The thought occurred to him that the people of the town might have need of it.

"It's so rusty, it's got to be abandoned, right?" Edward asked hopefully, his face grim.

Alphonse shook his head. "Hear those sounds from the town? They must still be excavating."

They stood absolutely still and they could hear sounds carried on the wind, sounds of machinery moving and of rocks being piled. Edward sighed. It seemed likely that the town still used that rusted crane, and it was a sure bet they wouldn't look kindly on the ones who had wrecked it. In his travels, Edward had found that it wasn't a good policy to make trouble upon arriving at your destination. Trouble was sure to come later, as it was.

"You really need to be more careful, Ed."

Edward's shoulders slumped. Bad enough that his little brother towered over him—now he was scolding him. "Guess we ought to fix it," Edward muttered, passing his traveling trunk to his brother.

"Why can't you ever learn to look but not touch?"

While his brother grumbled, Edward stood in front of the fallen crane and swiftly brought his hands together.

For a moment, it looked as if the air around the crane contracted. An instant later, the atmosphere around them snapped and vibrated, and light streamed everywhere.

"Good as new! Let's go, Al."

The light dissipated. Edward retrieved his trunk and began walking again. Alphonse hurried to catch up with him. Behind them, the crane stood exactly as it had when they arrived.

THE BROTHERS finally reached the town. Only a few dilapidated houses awaited them. The windowsills and foundations had turned the same dusty brown as the ground on which the buildings stood. At first Alphonse and Edward thought the place was abandoned, but when they reached the town center, they sensed activity. The sound of people's voices and breaking rocks echoed between the buildings. "Open" signs hung in shop windows, and they caught glimpses of rich goldware hanging on the walls inside.

"I was hoping this was the place." Edward's eyes followed a slow-moving rail cart. "So much gold was found here, I thought maybe . . . But this place looks pretty run down."

"Think we should move on?"

"No." Edward's eyes shone with determination. "We promised ourselves we'd check out every lead, every 'what if' and 'maybe,' and that's what we're going to do."

Alphonse nodded. "Okay."

"All right then."

They glanced at each other, then headed toward a building that stood in the middle of the town square. Its sign read "TAVERN." It had been a long journey, and they needed a rest.

The tavern held ten tables. A few grimy miners were drinking coffee inside. The brothers seated themselves, acknowledging the stares with a nod.

"Look, Al—goldware designs!" Edward pointed at inked schematics hanging on the walls. "Some rich guy somewhere must have the real things."

"Wow!" Alphonse exclaimed, genuinely impressed.

The designs were elegant and highly detailed. Edward imagined the finished objects must be priceless works of art. Though these were only the blueprints, they were enough to impress the travelers with the skill of the town's craftsmen.

"Whoa! Check out the price! That's one . . . No, ten . . ." Edward leaned closer to one of the pictures and studied the record of sale at the bottom. Slowly, he counted off zeros on his fingers. "Five million sens! For real!?"

While his brother counted off prices, Alphonse examined the designs. There were large bowls with fine detailing and small tables with short legs. To think that each of those black lines represented *solid gold!* Alphonse had no desire for such luxury, but the designs were exquisite. He looked over the largest one. Even without seeing the finished product, he could tell it was a masterpiece of craftsmanship.

"I guess I've always written off goldware as just some gaudy luxury for the rich."

"But it's a real art, isn't it?"

Alphonse turned to see who had said the words that had been forming on the tip of his tongue.

"What can I bring you, gentlemen?" continued the speaker, a rather tall man with a whiskered chin. He wore a cooking apron. Alphonse concluded he must be the tavern's proprietor. "Welcome, travelers! Those goldware designs are certainly something to look at, but if it's food you're after, my herbed chicken is a work of art in its own right!"

The man laughed easily, and the other patrons joined the conversation. "Better order the chicken! Can't rightly recommend anything else on the menu!" someone shouted, and the room filled with laughter.

"That stew the other day tasted like sawdust!"

"Ha! I tried it too—nearly lost a tooth!"

The man grinned. "I'll put together a few more recipes, just give me time." He plopped a coffee cup on the table. "So, you want the herbed chicken or what?"

Edward nodded. "All right. Does it come with bread?"

The man disappeared into the kitchen and returned to set their table. "You in the armor—anything for you?"

"I'm fine. Not hungry, thanks," Alphonse answered awkwardly. He couldn't eat even if he wanted to. He turned back to the designs. "These designs . . . Are they yours?"

The proprietor smiled. "Lemac's the name."

"Did you make these, Lemac?"

"Most of 'em. It's been a while, though. The bigger designs we made together."

"Wow! They're amazing!" breathed Alphonse.

"Thanks. Only rich folk can afford these, so most people think of 'em as indulgences. But one look at the designs, and most people agree they're art!"

Lemac brought a bowl and spoon and laid them on the table.

Edward pointed at the designs on the wall. "You just display your schematics in public like this?" The complexity of the designs defied belief. Wouldn't the goldsmiths want to keep them secret? Hung in the tavern like this, anyone could steal their patterns.

Lemac seemed unconcerned. "I didn't learn my craft in a day," he said with a grin. "Seeing isn't the same as smithing."

"Well, they're very beautiful. I didn't know people could work metal with such detail."

Alphonse's praise made Lemac blush. "Well, that was a long time ago."

"You don't make these anymore?"

Lemac's expression darkened. "You walked here from the

station, right? Did you see any mining carts in operation?"

"No." Alphonse shook his head. They had seen plenty of mining carts on their way in, but they were all rusting away.

Lemac turned to the window, a glass jar of herbs in his hand, and gazed out at the mines. Before the broken mountain was a wide plain. Several people crouched there, picking rocks from a pile and carefully examining them before tossing them aside.

"You can see we don't have enough gold or goldware to fill up even one mining cart these days. The rails to the station are all rusting. Used to be, you'd hear the sound of trains and blasting and digging all day long. The town was full of craftsmen and customers come to buy their work. It was an exciting place to be." His voice trailed off wistfully.

"Did the gold run out?" Edward asked.

"Appears so. There's signs of a fresh vein a ways down, but most folks will be long gone before we reach it. You can't grow crops on rock and sand."

"Uh-huh."

A palpable silence fell on the tavern. Lemac waved his hand as if to brush it away. "Well, I've got plenty of training left to do with my cooking arm if I ever want it to match my goldsmithing arm. Keeps me out of trouble all day."

A customer chimed in, "And by the time your cooking improves, we'll have found that gold!"

"That's right," another added. "And before we find that

gold, Mr. Mugear's research is bound to pan out!"

"I sure hope so . . ."

"What do you mean by that? We've just got to be patient! You want to craft gold again, don't you?"

Edward had been absentmindedly admiring the designs on the wall, but now his ears pricked up.

"Who's Mr. Mugear?"

"The owner of the mine. See that mansion up there? That's his place."

Just their side of the mountain, Edward saw a high wall with a large gate, firmly shut.

"That's a big house! He must make a fortune!"

"Mr. Mugear was the first to make a business venture out of the mine. But now that the gold's run dry, he's just as bad off as the rest of us. Things will turn around for all of us if his research works out, of course."

"Research?" Edward asked, trying to sound casual. He didn't want to appear too interested, even though the word "research" alone had started his heart racing.

"He's finished digging gold. He's trying to find a way to *make* it! As much as we want! He's manufacturing some kind of 'Philosopher's Stone.' "

Edward and Alphonse glanced at each other. This was the information they had been seeking. They were eager to ask more questions, but they were afraid of arousing suspicion. Reining in their curiosity, they listened attentively as Lemac talked on.

"You're not too young to have heard of alchemy, are you? Rumor has it if you're a good enough alchemist—the crème de la crème—you can make one of these stones. It's pretty high-level alchemy. Nobody knows if it's even possible."

"It is," asserted a man at the next table over. Several people nodded. Edward could see the hope in their eyes. They were all counting on this Mr. Mugear's success, that was clear.

Suddenly a dark voice sounded from a table in the corner. "It's impossible."

Everyone cast withering looks in the new speaker's direction. The man in the corner was spooning soup into his mouth. He looked as old or older than Lemac, and was sturdily built. He put his spoon down. His fingers were thick, and the face he turned to them was deeply tanned.

"How long have they been researching that 'Philosopher's Rock,' anyway? While they've been holed up in that laboratory with those alchemists-for-hire, our town is going to rack and ruin. Are we that obsessed with gold?"

A few people stood up and protested, their voices shrill in comparison to his deep baritone.

"We used to make goldware that was the rival of any in the land! Everyone knows the name of Xenotime! We can't just throw all that away!"

"That's right! We know there's another vein of gold out there. And a brilliant alchemist has joined Mr. Mugear's laboratory! They're bound to succeed! Belsio, you were never much of a craftsman yourself. Maybe you're willing to throw it all away, but we aren't!"

The man called Belsio slowly stood up. The atmosphere grew increasingly tense as he spoke in a soft voice. "Go on. Keep looking for your gold vein. But all we're doing is breaking up rocks and throwing them away. If they want to play mad scientist up at the manse, let them. But we don't have to keep funding their games with money we don't have." Belsio took a long look around the room. Then he placed the payment for his meal on the table and walked out, leaving the other patrons to digest his words.

"These are bad times for all of us! That's why we're scraping our money together to fund Mugear's research. That Belsio's just a naysayer."

"Mugear's collaborating with lots of alchemists. If anyone can make a stone that'll turn rocks into gold, it's him. And then we can all go back to trying to outdo each other's goldware again!"

"But shouldn't we at least consider some alternatives!?"

"What's wrong with you? You'd throw away goldsmithing just like that?"

"I don't want to throw anything away. But my son's not well, and I'm thinking of moving and taking up a new profession. I'm stagnating in this town."

"But if you stay, eventually—"

"Now, now," broke in Lemac, "talk won't solve anything. We've just got to keep busy. Norris, you've been searching for an expert to help find that gold vein, right? How's that going? We've got to get back to mining! Delfino, don't you have an order for goldware to fill?"

Lemac worked his way around the room, clapping several people on the back. The man he spoke to last had been Belsio's harshest critic. "You're right," the man said, rising from his seat.

Lemac turned to Edward. "Delfino is the best craftsman in town. He's got some smaller pieces that aren't too expensive. You should take a look. There's not much else to see here."

"Thank you," Edward said, "but what I'd really like to see is Mr. Mugear's laboratory."

Lemac and the others, many of whom were on their way out the door, stopped in their tracks. They laughed at the boy's serious tone.

"You're barely older than my daughter!" Lemac said, tousling Edward's hair. "Are you really interested in all that nerdy alchemy stuff?"

To Lemac, Edward was nothing but a boy, and alchemy was an impossibly technical science. The townspeople's hopes all rested on it, but they never dreamed of comprehending it.

"The laboratory is off-limits. Not even *we* are allowed inside," one of the men said. "First time I've met a kid interested in alchemy," he added. "Your dad get you started?"

Everyone looked at bronze-armored Alphonse, who was standing beside Edward.

"Huh?" Alphonse sputtered, not following their point.

Edward gave him a dirty look. This was a new one. "What!?" Alphonse glared at his brother.

"Sorry," Edward said. He laughed. "It's just, that's the first time someone's mistaken you for my dad!"

The unlikely pair of a short boy and a giant suit of armor had been mistaken for a variety of things by a variety of people. It was only natural to assume that the taller one in the armor was the older of the two. And if they didn't introduce themselves as brothers right away, people leapt to all sorts of conclusions. They had been taken for wandering troubadours, a legendary pair of rogues, a boy from a royal estate and his knightly guardian—but never before for a father and son.

"He's not your father?" the man asked. He seemed taken aback by Alphonse's response. He glanced at Edward, who smiled.

"We're brothers," Edward said, enunciating clearly.

"'Brothers'!?"

"Really!?"

"It's true," Alphonse said. "We actually look a lot alike."

"I guess your voices do sound similar."

"Sorry!"

"No problem," Alphonse said, waving away the apology with his armored hand. "Happens all the time."

"Well, I'm still sorry I called you his dad!" the man said, reaching over to slap Alphonse on the shoulder. "You've probably got enough to worry about watching out for your little brother without being taken for his father!"

A long silence.

Finally Edward said—a little too loudly—"He's *my* little brother!"

The crowd was surprised again.

No matter how many times this happened, it never failed to get on Edward's nerves. Alphonse gave him a sidelong glance and sighed. Having compounded misunderstanding upon misunderstanding, the townspeople didn't know what to say.

"Daddy, I'm home!" A bright voice cut through the tension.

"Welcome back, Elisa!" Lemac spread his arms and a little girl flew into them.

"This is my daughter, Elisa. Elisa, say hello to our guests."

The girl turned around. "Hello!"

Edward waved, and Elisa's eyes grew big. "Hey, it's that alchemist boy!" she shouted. Once again, the townspeople were startled.

"What did you say, Elisa?"

Elisa turned to her father, her eyes sparkling. "He knocked over our crane, but then he used alchemy to fix it! I saw the whole thing. There was a big flash of light. It was so pretty!"

Lemac looked at Edward, the doubt in his eyes plain to see. "You're an alchemist?"

It wasn't something Edward had to hide, but he was

suddenly wary of revealing too much. "Sort of."

"And that's why you're interested in the lab?"

"That's right," Edward replied. Quickly, before anyone else could say it, he added, "I know it's hard to believe someone so young could be an alchemist." He'd told people of his abilities a hundred times, but most adults didn't believe him. To his surprise, however, no one in the tavern seemed to doubt him at all. Instead, hope shone on their faces.

"Really? You're an alchemist? Then you should go to Mugear's lab right away!"

"Huh?" Edward was stunned by their sudden change in attitude.

"You can help them make the Philosopher's Stone! Do you know how? That's okay, even if you don't, you might be able to nudge them in the right direction!"

The townspeople took turns shaking Edward's hand.

"To think you can perform alchemy at such a young age. You know what they say about a youthful imagination, though! You should go!"

"Please! For us!"

The men continued to urge the two to go to the laboratory as soon as possible. They seemed to respect them now.

"Well, Al? What should we do?"

"I guess we better check out the lab!"

Finding the Philosopher's Stone was the goal of their journey, and if this team of researchers was working on creating one from scratch, there was no question of their eagerness to see it. They would have found a way to sneak into the lab, if necessary. To be openly invited was a stroke of luck.

"All right," Edward agreed.

The men smiled warmly, perhaps in response to the gleam of excitement in Edward's eyes.

"I'm sure a fresh perspective will do those researchers a world of good."

"There seem to be a lot of young alchemists these days," Lemac said. "There's one up at the laboratory right now."

"Really?" Edward said, his curiosity piqued. Alchemists as young as himself were few and far between. "How old is this one?"

"How old are you?"

"Fifteen. My brother, Alphonse, is fourteen."

"You're kidding!"

Everyone looked Edward up and down from head to toe. He knew what they were thinking. Alphonse looked on anxiously, hoping the townspeople wouldn't mention his brother's height.

"Fifteen! You look so much younger!"

"Aye! Seems alchemists are getting younger and younger these days. The one up at the laboratory is around the same age, isn't he?

"He's my age? Really?"

"So tell us, boys," Lemac said, refilling their coffee cups, "what are your names?"

Edward nodded his thanks for the coffee. "Our name's Elric. I'm Edward, and this is Alphonse."

Everyone stiffened. The atmosphere in the room shifted.

"What was that?"

It was a surname that anyone who knew anything about alchemy was bound to have heard before. Edward was used to the look of shock when he introduced himself and Alphonse as the famous Elric brothers. This time seemed no different, so without a second thought, he repeated himself.

"I'm Edward Elric."

This time he was greeted not by surprise, but peals of laughter.

"You're Edward Elric? Do you really think you can impersonate him?!"

"Aren't you a little old to be telling fibs, boy?"

Edward stuttered. "'B-boy'!?"

"It's understandable that you'd envy him. Master Edward is a State Alchemist, after all."

The townspeople said his name—"Master Edward"—as though they knew him!

"What do you mean by that?"

"You gave us a good laugh, lad," Lemac said. His voice had suddenly grown a little cold. "Now tell us your real name."

Nobody believed Edward. He repeated himself until the

townspeople looked as though they'd heard enough.

Lemac scowled, gazing down at Edward as if he were a recalcitrant child. "I understand why a boy would want to emulate his hero, but there's such a thing as going too far. If you were any older, I'd knock a little sense into you right here and now."

Elisa looked sadly at the two brothers.

"What's your problem!" sputtered Edward.

Lemac ignored his outburst. "Look, you think on this son, and come back when you're ready to tell us your real names." He pointed toward the door. When they didn't move, he guided Alphonse and Edward out of the tavern, and tossed their traveling trunk out onto the street after them.

"I told you my name! My real name! I'm Edward Elric!"

"And I'm Alphonse Elric," added Alphonse meekly.

No one listened.

A voice drifted out from the tavern. "I thought there was something strange about those two from the start!"

"What!?" Edward shouted. "What's gotten into you people!? We aren't lying! I'm Edward and this is Alphonse. He's my brother! Why won't you believe us?"

"Ed, wait!" Alphonse held his brother back. He knew Edward was spoiling for a fight, and that was the last thing he wanted.

"Let go of me, Al!"

"Wait," Alphonse repeated. He turned to the small

crowd gathered at the tavern door. "Listen, this is all a misunderstanding. We really are the Elric brothers. I know it's hard to believe, but it's true."

It was a noble effort, but Edward grabbed Alphonse's arm and yanked him back. "Let's go, Al. I don't want to talk to these idiots anymore."

"Ed!"

"What do you expect me to do?" Edward continued, not caring who heard him. "We're telling the truth, and they don't want to hear it! We'll just go on our way. If we want to go to the lab, we'll go to the lab."

"Was that it, son?" Lemac asked. "You lied to us so you could see the laboratory? If you'd just told us your true names, we'd have let you go."

Edward glared at him. "We told you our true names. It's not our problem you won't believe us."

As Edward picked up their traveling trunk, Alphonse handed money to Lemac. "For the food. Thank you."

Lemac sighed. His disappointment was palpable. He had hoped these boys could provide a breakthrough in the town's alchemy research.

"I wish you'd had a better lie," Lemac said. "But claiming to be the Elrics . . . !?" He pushed the other customers back inside.

"Why are you so convinced we're lying!?"

Lemac turned around. "Because the Elric brothers are

already at the laboratory."

He quietly shut the door and left them standing in the street, dumbfounded.

EDWARD AND ALPHONSE sat under a withered tree on the outskirts of town. They looked at each other, and Edward scratched his head.

"What's going on?" Alphonse asked after a long silence. "How could we already be here, Ed?"

"It's obvious. The laboratory needed alchemists. Someone must have pretended to be us to get in." Edward picked up a dry stick. "People know me because of my title, but they don't know my face. It's the perfect cover if you want to sneak into a lab." Edward began to scribble on the ground with the stick.

Alphonse watched. A simple diagram, surrounded by a list of everything they knew about the Philosopher's Stone.

Glows red.

Incredibly dense.

Unlimited alchemical power.

The words were randomly arranged. This was all the information they had gathered on their journey. For all their dreams of the Stone, they had never seen the real thing.

Alphonse knew well what his brother was thinking. "Ed, you're going to break into Mugear's lab, aren't you?"

Edward stared at the diagram he had drawn in the dirt.

"We've been searching for so long . . . " His voice was quiet and steady. "I'll get you back your body."

The Philosopher's Stone was like the diagram he had drawn: a dream, a thing of the imagination. A light wind blew across the sand, and slowly, the drawing of the Stone faded away.

"I'll get the real thing," Edward said with determination. He stood up. "After it gets dark, we're going, Al."

"What about the other Elric brothers?"

"We leave 'em be."

Edward didn't think much of the impostors. He began searching for a vantage point from which to view the Mugear estate. Winning the title of State Alchemist had been only one step toward his ultimate goal: creating a Philosopher's Stone so he could return his brother to his human form. Compared to the Stone, some jokers posing as him and Alphonse were of little concern.

"Just . . . leave them be?"

"Sure. Doesn't sound like they've done anything bad in our names." Edward pointed at a nearby rise. "Hey, we might be able to see better from that hill up there."

"Don't you think impersonating us is bad enough?"

The two walked toward the hill. As they approached, they realized it was artificial—just a pile of unearthed stone. In fact, all the hills surrounding the town in every direction were just heaps of stone, left over from years of mining. When the brothers reached the crest of the heap they were aiming for, they looked down at the town. From their position, they could see that of all the town's buildings, the Mugear mansion was the largest by far. Furthermore, it was the only one surrounded by a wall—and a high one at that.

"Looks like there's only one entrance. There are guards, too. We'll have to go over the wall," Edward declared.

"The other side is fenced off too. Looks like barbed wire."

They strained to get a better a look until they heard a rock falling below them. They looked down to see a man squatting at the bottom of the mound. He picked up a heavy-looking stone and placed it in the mining cart beside him. It was Belsio, the man who had questioned the townspeople's dependence on the outcome of the alchemy research.

"You're Belsio, right? What are you doing?" Edward called from atop the rock pile.

"Clearing rocks. What's it look like?" Belsio answered gruffly without pausing. He lifted another and placed it in the cart. "You know, it's not safe up there," he added, without looking up. "Never can tell when there's going to be a rockslide."

The two heeded his warning and carefully made their way down until they stood beside him. Edward peered into his mining cart. It was already half full of stones.

"What are you going to do with all these stones?"

Belsio pointed to a small, neatly fashioned stone wall nearby. "There's a little pond over there, but the dirt keeps sliding into it. I'm going to make a rim like that around it with these rocks."

"By yourself?"

"Yep. I'm the only one using that now." He indicated a lone waterway trickling out from the pond towards a small field bordered with stones.

"A vegetable patch," Alphonse said. He noticed several small, red objects amongst the greenery. "Tomatoes! So you've given up goldsmithing, Belsio?"

"With no gold to work, I can't live by my craft anymore. Had to find something else to do. I'm only providing for myself now, but eventually I'll grow enough vegetables to sell. It wasn't an easy choice to make, mind you."

Belsio raised his head and looked the brothers in the eyes for the first time. "A long time ago, the soil here was rich and fertile and the water was clear. There was even a river. It wasn't much, but we had a good, quiet life. But now . . . Look at this place! Once they found gold, everything changed. The town was going to buy the rights to the mine so everyone could have a share in it, but Mugear bought up all the mining rights for himself.

"He piled the cut rock and sand right up to the borders of his land. The dust from his rock piles blew into his neighbor's fields and ruined them. They couldn't make a living off the land anymore, so they sold it all off to him, and he piled more rocks on it. Eventually, there wasn't any arable land

left anywhere. With that and the gold money pouring in, prices went through the roof. Eventually everyone had to work in the mines to survive. They called in top artisans to teach goldsmithing. We took our craft seriously, and we got good at it fast."

Belsio had a far-off look in his eyes as he recalled the days of the gold rush, but when he turned once again to face the rock pile, his expression turned bitter.

"It went bad in the blink of an eye. No matter how many times you clean up a piece of land, sand just blows back onto it from that mountain. My orchards won't grow. So now we don't have gold *or* green. And still people can't see what's happening. They're betting everything on a dream—that Philosopher's Stone."

Edward looked out at the dry, dusty land. As Belsio had said, there was nothing green or gold as far as the eye could see, except for Belsio's tiny vegetable patch. "So everyone's counting on the Philosopher's Stone to save your town?"

"They say it's a miracle maker. That it can turn these cold rocks lying here into pure gold. We know there's more gold deeper down, but it'll take a long time to get to it. Mugear is desperate to keep eating until then—and to be as rich as he used to be. He's got everyone throwing money at his fool's plan."

"Why would they invest in something that might not even be possible?" Alphonse asked.

"When they built the lab, they had a real big-shot alchemist working up there. He was the student of some famous alchemist from the central labs. When they came to town looking for investors he made gold for us, right before our eyes."

"What!?"

Belsio waved Edward's amazement off.

"It was just temporary. The stones glittered like gold for a few seconds, then crumbled to dust."

Edward was silent.

"Still, it was enough to give everyone a shred of hope," Belsio continued. "The alchemist told everyone he was on the verge of perfecting his technique, and they came up with the money he asked for. Mugear is in the same boat as we are. He won't sell out to competitors who put offers on his mansion and the mine. He won't let go of our golden age."

"Where's that alchemist now?" Edward asked eagerly. Although his experiments had ended in failure, they might provide him with valuable clues. If they could talk to this scientist, they might get some solid leads. The central alchemical labs were known for their talented researchers. But what Belsio said next dashed Edward's hopes.

"He's not here anymore. He just took off one day. To hear Mugear tell it, he was ashamed of his failure. 'Course, I think he just got sick of Mugear pushing him around."

"Oh," Edward said, disappointed.

"When he left, the research screeched to a halt. It would have been better for everyone if we'd just given up then, but someone came along to pick up where he left off, someone with an incredible reputation. He came trotting into town and made friends quick, fixing broken tools and the like. Real popular, that one."

The false Edward Elric.

Belsio looked at Edward. "You've got the same name, is that it?" he asked bluntly.

"He's an impostor," Edward sneered, certain Belsio wouldn't believe him.

Belsio seemed unfazed. "Folks are on edge these days. They're good people, really—not the type who'd normally get so up in arms against a kid. Listen, if you can't stay at the tavern, you're welcome at my place."

"Do you believe us, Belsio?"

"Hey, I figure everyone's got their life to live. You're responsible for yourself and your business isn't any of mine."

It seemed he did believe them or, at least, that he didn't care if they were lying. For what it was worth, he wasn't leaving them to sleep on the street.

WHILE EDWARD AND ALPHONSE talked with Belsio on the rockpile, a crowd of people were gathering in front of Lemac's tavern. They carried broken tools in their arms.

"Can you fix this, Master Edward?"

"Please look at my pick."

"Master Edward!"

In the middle of the circle of men stood a blond boy. He waved his hands for silence. "Don't worry. Everyone will get a turn."

He placed a broken rock pick on a table before him and spread out his hands. There was a bright flash of light, and the pick was as good as new.

"Thank you, Master Edward!" gushed the man standing on the other side of the table.

The boy smiled and handed him the pick. "Take care."

This was young Master Edward. His wavy blond hair was cut short and hung over eyes of a nearly transparent blue that shone silver in the light. He was clearly in his teens, but his strong physique and the ease with which he spoke to the grown men around him made him seem much older. The townspeople were grateful for his help and treated him with great respect as he used his alchemy to fix one tool after another. This charismatic youth fit their image of a child prodigy and State Alchemist far better than the real Edward ever could have.

Toward the rear of the line of supplicants waiting to have the impostor examine their broken tools and machinery stood another boy inspecting a broken chisel. He was shorter than the other, but similar in appearance, with the same golden hair, silver-blue eyes, and short hair. This was the boy who called himself Alphonse.

"Ah, this is just bent here. Don't worry, you'll get your turn soon." The false Alphonse glanced worriedly at the crowd. "Please be patient just a little longer."

The owner of the chisel grinned. "I'll wait as long as it takes. I've had this fixed quite a few times already, actually. The spot I'm digging at is hard bedrock, and it keeps breaking my chisel."

"I see . . . Sorry I'm not much help myself." Alphonse returned the chisel, casting a glance at his busy brother.

"Nonsense, Master Alphonse. You assist Master Edward with his work. We don't all have to be alchemists to be useful, you know."

Suddenly, the false Edward noticed him holding the chisel. "Alphonse," he called out, "don't touch that. You'll hurt yourself."

It was meant kindly, but it made "Alphonse" jump.

"Bring that over here."

"O-okay."

The chisel was fixed in a moment. "Edward" checked it over carefully with sure fingers and returned it to its owner.

"Sorry for the wait. I know you've got lots of mining to do."

"You're doing the best you can. We're honored you take time out of your research to help us fix our tools."

"Unfortunately, this is all I can do without the Stone." Edward turned back to the crowd. "Next?"

The man named Delfino approached and handed him a small bag.

"Master Edward, this is from all of us. It's not much, but I hope it'll help you with your research."

Coins clinked and jangled as he laid the bag down gently on the table.

Edward frowned. "I know times are hard for all of you . . ."

Delfino brushed away his protest with a gesture. "Please don't worry about us, Master Edward. The research you're doing is for our benefit. It's the least we can do to support your work."

"Well, thank you, then. I'll be sure to let Mr. Mugear know about your contribution. And just you watch—once we make the Stone, we'll return your investment a hundredfold!" Edward put away the bag. "It won't be long now. We're giving it our all."

"Take care to pace yourselves, Master Edward, Master Alphonse," Delfino said, nodding to each of the brothers in turn.

"Thank you," Edward replied.

"We're all counting on you."

The townspeople shook his hand and Edward ducked his head humbly to acknowledge their words of thanks. Watching him, Delfino whispered to Lemac, "Master Edward is a wonderful boy. I can see why those travelers would be tempted to impersonate him."

Lemac nodded. "I agree."

Edward overheard them. "What's this about some travelers?"

Lemac and Delfino laughed, recalling the scene in the tavern.

"Oh, it's nothing," Lemac said. "Two travelers—boys, really—came into town today, and when we asked their names, they said they were the Elric brothers!"

"Two boys?"

"Yes, but the one who said he was Edward was much younger than you, Master Edward, and the one who said he was Alphonse was hidden inside a big suit of armor. To think they'd pretend to be the famous Elrics! They don't even look like brothers. You must get that a lot, though. I suppose you have a lot of starry-eyed fans."

Lemac and Delfino laughed. They missed the ripple of tension running across Edward's face.

"Did they know alchemy?"

"Elisa claims she saw them use it, but I doubt it. She must have been mistaken."

Lemac picked Elisa up and held her in his arms.

"It's true!" Elisa said, pouting. "I saw a light flash when he fixed the crane. Just like when Master Edward rescued me!"

Patting his stubborn daughter on the head, Lemac smiled ruefully. "It seems both of them are interested in alchemy. I'm afraid all their talk must have gone to Elisa's head. In any case, they gave up their pretense and left. I guess they just wanted to play at being their heroes. Boys will be boys!"

"Yes . . ." Edward trailed off.

"I think they're still in town," added Lemac. "I told them to come back when they were ready to tell us their real names."

Edward put his hand to his chin, apparently deep in thought.

Delfino raised an eyebrow. "Something wrong?"

"No," Edward said, his easy smile returning. "I was just thinking what an honor it is to be considered a hero."

The men laughed.

"Well," Edward said nonchalantly, "I guess we better get back to the lab. If you see those two posers again, don't pay them any mind."

The impostor of Alphonse gave the impostor of Edward a worried glance, but said nothing.

As they headed back toward Mugear's mansion, Alphonse, walking behind his brother, broke the silence.

"Isn't this going to be a problem for us?"

"How so?" Edward asked, smiling as he waved to passersby.

Alphonse started to say something, but nothing came out.

The boy who called himself Edward turned around. "You want to tell them *we're* the impostors, is that it?"

Alphonse nodded.

Edward put his arm around his younger brother's shoulder and gave him a hearty shake. "Listen, what's our goal?"

"To create the Philosopher's Stone and save the town."

"Right. And we've already managed to make a prototype!" He patted his chest pocket. "We're so close! We can't give up now!"

"But—"

"But what? Look, no one suspects we're anyone other than the real Elric brothers."

"But if Mr. Mugear hears about this, he'll look into it. What if something goes wrong? What if we get arrested and prosecuted!?"

"That's why we have to make sure the real brothers don't meet Mugear. They must be after the Stone . . . or us. Either way, they'll try to get into the lab."

"So what do we do?"

"Isn't it obvious?" He patted his chest pocket. "I'll fight them. With this."

THE NIGHT WORE ON and the patrons drinking at Lemac's tavern shuffled home. One by one, the lights of the town went out.

Around midnight, when most of the townspeople were sleeping quietly in their beds, two shadows cut across town.

"Al! This way!" Edward whispered. He was crouched beneath the wall that ran around the Mugear mansion.

Alphonse ran over from the other side of the road, and they sat with their backs to the wall.

"Well?"

"The front entrance is a no-go, like we thought. There are three guards."

"Well, I didn't see any other entrances," Alphonse said. "I guess we'll have to go up and over."

They gazed at the wall, bathed in moonlight. It stood about fifteen feet high. Edward stepped out a few steps into the street and turned to face it. Alphonse held out his hands, his fingers joined. Without a moment's hesitation, Edward ran full speed toward him. Stepping onto Alphonse's outstretched hands, he launched himself into the air. At the same moment, Alphonse thrust his hands upward, sending Edward soaring.

This was a familiar maneuver of theirs—they'd had many opportunities to perfect it. Most of the time, they were sneaking into someone's house, like now, or trespassing at some facility. It wasn't something they were proud of, really, but rather a testament to the hard road they traveled that made this the best-honed stunt in their repertoire. Still, as practiced as they were, it was a difficult maneuver to pull off, and they sometimes miscalculated.

Alphonse grimaced. Edward was only barely hanging on to the far edge of the wall, holding himself up with one leg hooked over the top.

"Al, you threw me too far," he hissed.

"Sorry! You didn't eat dinner." Alphonse grabbed onto the wire that Edward lowered to him. He was being nice. If Edward weren't his brother, he would have told the truth—that Edward was just too light.

Both atop the wall now, they surveyed the situation on the inside of the estate grounds. When they were satisfied no one could see them, they used the wire to lower themselves to the ground. They had successfully infiltrated the grounds. They sat motionless. No guards were forthcoming.

"Looks like we pulled it off."

"Yeah."

They breathed a sigh of relief and took a look around. The courtyard they found themselves in was very wide. Trees filled the premises, a rich green that contrasted sharply with the parched foliage outside. Perhaps the high wall protected them from the choking sands that had claimed the rest of the town's vegetation. Beyond the shadows of the leaves they could make out the large mansion.

The brothers set off, weaving through the trees. Soon they came to the end of the trees and the three-story mansion became visible.

"I wonder where the lab is," Alphonse whispered.

"It's hard to imagine they'd use a regular room. They probably need chemicals and fire for their experiments. They'd want a place where they can control the temperature."

Edward studied the building. From where they stood, they could easily grasp the layout of the place: a four-cornered box with a large, open corridor cutting into the front and windows set high in the walls. On the back wall the windows were evenly spaced, perhaps indicating a row of similarly sized rooms. On one corner, a room protruded from the rest of the building. It seemed to have only one small window.

"There! Found it!" Edward pointed.

"Look at that room. Someone added it on after the rest of the building was finished. It's pretty big, but there's only one window. And look at that chimney. Everyone must be asleep by now, but there's smoke coming out of it."

Alphonse nodded.

"Makes sense. You've got to run experiments night and day when you're doing alchemy. Come on, let's go see how far they've come!"

The two moved around to the far side. A light shone from the small laboratory window.

"Someone's still up?" Alphonse wondered.

"I doubt it. I bet it's just a fire they're burning to keep their experiments at a constant temperature." Edward turned to Alphonse. "If someone's in there, we'll lure them out. And then you can take them away."

"Where?"

"Anywhere away from here."

Their voices low, the brothers plotted their strategy.

"And if no one's home," Edward went on, "we pick the lock or break in. Once we're inside, go for the research data first. Even if they've got a prototype stone in there, we'll never know how they're refining it just by looking at it. Better to review their notes."

"And if they do have a Philosopher's Stone?"

"I doubt they've completed one. But even if they have, we leave it. If we steal something that valuable and they trace it to us, we'll be in big trouble."

"But if we just read their notes, they won't have any proof and they can't track us, right?"

"Exactly. All we need to do is get a list of their materials and a grasp of their alchemical process. Then we can make one ourselves. It would leave a bad taste in my mouth to steal the Stone the townspeople have been waiting for all this time."

"Me too."

The boys wanted the Stone so badly it hurt, but they couldn't steal the town's only hope. Even if they broke a few rules sometimes, they never intended anybody any harm.

"Run fast . . ." Edward said.

"Open the door . . ." Alphonse continued.

"Find those research notes . . ."

". . . and read 'em all as quick as we can!"

"Right!"

"Very interesting," observed a voice from above.

The brother's heads whipped up. Someone was looking down on them, his arms folded across his chest.

"I see," he said. "A bold plan, yet low impact. I approve."

They hadn't noticed their observer, and he didn't seem the least bit concerned that they were intruders. Now they could make out a smaller figure standing behind him—a boy. Edward and Alphonse looked at one another. Slowly, they stood up and stepped back. Their observer stared at them calmly.

"So," Edward said in a low voice, "who the heck are you?"

Their observer guffawed. "You're the ones who are trespassing. I'd like to ask you the same question."

Edward studied him. On closer examination, he didn't appear to be that much older than Edward himself. And the fact that he didn't seem surprised to have discovered Edward and Alphonse could only mean that he had been expecting them. Silver eyes with the faintest tinge of blue studied Edward in return. This must be the one they had heard about, the alchemist around Edward's age who worked at the laboratory.

"You're the impostor who's pretending to be me!" Edward declared, daring him to deny it.

"It's hard to get into a lab when you're as young as I am. We needed names. Big names. As luck would have it, a certain

Edward Elric became a State Alchemist at a very young age. Your hard work did wonders opening doors for us. We owe you our thanks."

"'Thanks!?'" Edward couldn't believe it. He had admitted to it—and worse, now he was politely thanking him! "People are treating us like liars because of you! Look, your game is up! Tell everyone the truth!"

Edward was the one who had said they were there for the Philosopher's Stone and that they should forget about the impostors, but now that those impostors stood right in front of him, he was furious.

The impostor smiled. "Sorry, but that's not going to happen. I still need your name."

"What!?"

"Just keep playing the part of the impostor for me for a while, okay?"

"*You're* the one who's gonna be in parts, buddy!"

Compared to steaming Edward, the impostor remained cool and collected.

"Listen," he said, still smiling, "I've conducted myself in a manner befitting a State Alchemist. We've been careful not to tarnish your name. Why, you might say I've got a better reputation than you do!"

Edward was speechless.

"In fact," the impostor continued, "when I first used your name, the townspeople wondered if we were those ill-mannered rapscallions they'd heard tell of!"

"Yeah, because they knew you weren't the real thing!"

"What I'm saying is, don't worry. I'm going to improve your image!"

"What!?" snorted Edward.

Behind them, Alphonse rolled his eyes. "Ed, he's playing you. Calm down, will you?"

From behind the false Edward, the smaller boy spoke.

"Why do you always do that to people . . . say things to make them mad?"

In mirror image, both older brothers had been chastised by their younger siblings. They fell silent. This was no time to start a comedy routine.

The two Edwards glared at each other silently, until the real Edward finally remembered his goal and took off his jacket. This impostor stood between him and vital research on the Philosopher's Stone. And, more importantly, Edward really wanted to hit something.

"*I'm* Edward Elric, and this is my brother, Alphonse," he said, emphasizing the *I'm*. "I'll make you confess to your real name in front of the whole town if I have to make you crawl on the ground first."

The impostor didn't quake. "Now there's no need to resort to violence if you want my real name. It's Russell. And this is my brother, Fletcher."

"You *are* a bold one, aren't you?" sneered Edward. "I'll be sure to pass those names on to Mugear and the townspeople."

"Go ahead. No one will believe you."

"Wha—!?" Edward stammered.

"After all, I'm more like the real thing than you are."

"*What!?*"

"I've got character, I've got compassion, I've got the confidence of a genius alchemist, and I've got style."

"'Style'!" roared Edward. "Says who!?"

Behind him, Alphonse groaned. It was true—no one would ever mistake his brother for an elite State Alchemist. In fact, if someone had to choose between the real Edward and the impostor, they would probably pick the fake.

Edward was aware of this too. His anger at the impostor only grew because he played the role better than Edward himself.

"I'm not going to get this out of my system without getting in a good punch. Alphonse, we'll find the research data after we deal with him."

"I was afraid of this . . ." Alphonse swallowed and took a few steps back. When things came to blows, Alphonse usually felt it was best to get out of the way.

"I'll see whether you've got what it takes to call yourself a State Alchemist!" Edward shouted. He pressed his hands together. It looked as if he was about to perform alchemy, but then he stepped forward.

Russell kept his eyes on Edward's hands, ready for the alchemical attack that was sure to come. He was so focused that the fist that swooped up nearly caught him. As it was, he dodged the blow by a hair.

Edward smiled. "It takes strength to be a State Alchemist. You didn't think I'd rely on my alchemy alone in a fight, did you?" The hard journey and daily sparring practice with Alphonse had polished his fighting arm. He was confident he had the upper hand. Russell looked frail and unprepared for a fistfight. But he laughed and patted his ear as if to erase the sound of the near miss.

"Fine. I'm up for a fight, and I can't stand being made fun of."

It didn't look like Russell was preparing himself, but when he kicked, the foot came flying at Edward's head faster than Edward could have imagined. Edward blocked with his arm. The kick was stronger than he could have imagined, too.

Edward shook the numbness out of his arm. That hadn't gone as expected, but lots of guys seemed stronger than they really were on the first strike, and he took Russell for one of those. Besides, after his kick, Russell was off balance. Edward lunged forward and grabbed Russell's arm with his left hand. Curling his empty hand into a fist, he thrust at the impostor's chest. If the blow landed, he would momentarily knock the wind out of Russell. That would buy him time to land two or three more punches to finish him. Or so he thought . . . For once again, Edward underestimated his opponent.

Russell twisted his pinned arm quickly and freed himself,

then swung a fist at the side of Edward's face. At the same time, he caught Edward's fist in the palm of his other hand— just as Edward caught his.

Edward bit his lip and glared at Russell. His opponent was slender, but he was strong, that much was clear from his grip. Edward never thought he'd meet his equal in a boy his own age.

Gripping one another's fists, the two boys stood glaring at each other at point-blank range. Neither would yield, and their strength was nearly even. Russell looked at Edward's left hand, which was enclosed around his fist.

"Your hand's cold. I see you've had your share of problems." Russell had evidently noticed that the hand was auto-mail. A glance at Edward's left leg was enough to tell him that it was auto-mail, too.

Edward grimaced. "Yeah, but you didn't get this strong lying around on some beach your whole life, either."

Even as they talked, little by little, Edward's fist was being pulled upward. With the two standing so close, it was clear that Russell was more than a head taller than Edward. They had both swung their fists straight, but while Russell's was aimed for Edward's face, Edward's was aimed at Russell's chest. If Russell pulled his fist any higher, Edward would be reaching, and the balance of strength would tip against him.

Russell's methods weren't showy, but they spoke of

plenty of hands-on experience. What's more, it seemed he had strength to spare. As he saw Russell smiling down at him, Edward realized for the first time that he was at a disadvantage.

"You're not the only one who's had a tough life."

"So it seems."

Though it irked them, they had agreed on something, and with that as a signal, they both let go.

Edward stepped back and brought his hands together. It was alchemy time. "Time to take this fight to the streets!" he shouted, suddenly thrusting a hand onto the stone tiles of the courtyard. "I want to see this lab of yours, and this is how I'll do it!"

It looked as though the very air around the tile twitched and hardened. In an instant, the material of the tile broke apart and reformed. When the invisible twisting stopped, a wall grew from the ground, pulled upward by Edward's rising hand. He pulled until the wall was as tall as he was, then slapped his flat palm against it, causing the opposite side to bulge. The bulge formed the material of the wall into several conical shapes—spikes that shot toward Russell with the speed of Edward's thrusting hand. As they shot towards him, the wall grew smaller, like a living thing that had undergone a metamorphosis into hard, stinging tentacles.

"Fly!" Edward shouted, sending the continually elongating spikes at his opponent. Russell was no newcomer to such battles, so he would dodge—which was why Edward made sure he sent a few extra spikes for insurance.

"Impressive! You didn't even need to draw a transmutation circle!"

Russell was genuinely impressed. But although his eyes shone with amazement, he didn't seem flustered. "You really are a State Alchemist," he observed as he put his hand onto the courtyard.

Now it was Edward's turn to be surprised. Just as Edward had done, the impostor drew a wall of material from the courtyard tiles. The spears that erupted from his wall struck the ones Edward had propelled towards him, and as they collided in midair, they splintered into nothing.

The battle ended in a matter of seconds. However, it had been more than long enough for each combatant to gauge the other's strength.

Edward fixed Russell with a steady gaze.

They used the exact same methods. Their strength was evenly matched. Neither used a transmutation circle of power. Both had performed a feat far above the ability of the average alchemist.

This was no run-of-the-mill dabbler in alchemy Edward was facing. He had talent, the strength to rival an alchemist many called a genius . . . Or else . . .

A light dawned in Edward's face.

Russell laughed.

"You have it, don't you?"

In answer to Edward's half-whispered question, Russell put his hand into his breast pocket. His fingertips reached inside and dug around, searching. Under Edward's steely gaze, he drew something out and held it between his thumb and index finger.

A red shard.

It was small and so translucent it seemed it might shatter at any moment. It was a beautiful thing, sparkling in the moonlight.

"The Philosopher's Stone . . . "

This was what Edward was searching for. The legendary Stone, able to break the laws of alchemy. The real deal.

"You completed it?"

"Merely a trial version."

"And that's how you can fight me like this?"

Russell's rudimentary alchemical abilities had been magnified by the power of the prototype he carried. He glanced at Edward. "Like I said, it's just a trial stone. You want it?"

"Of course!" Edward didn't have to think about his answer. Just imagine the clues he could wring from that Stone, with a little luck!

"Of course you do. Too bad I'm not gonna give it to you." Russell put the Stone back in his pocket.

"I've made a bunch of these, but they're of limited use.

They'll have to be much, much better before I can make gold that will last instead of crumbling to dust. That's why I have to continue my research. And that's why you need to leave. Now."

"Not going to happen."

"Really? Linger any longer, and Mr. Mugear might begin to suspect something."

"Sounds like *your* problem," Edward spat.

"Too bad." Russell sighed. "I suppose this calls for more forceful tactics."

Edward braced for action. "I'll take that Stone, and I'll make you confess in front of the whole town!"

"I won't give you the Stone, and I'll prove I'm better than the real thing!"

Simultaneously, each boy grabbed courtyard tiles that had broken off during the previous fight. Light from alchemical reactions sparked in the air as massive stone swords formed in both of their hands.

"I'll beat an apology out of that big mouth of yours!"

"I'll have you crying for mercy long before that!"

"Hah!"

"Hah!"

An instant later, they flew at each other and struck.

Alphonse watched, all the while gauging the distance between himself and the lab. He had hoped to slip by while his brother fought the impostor, but the chances were looking slim. Russell fought with his back to the laboratory, and if Alphonse passed him, he'd be sure to take a hit. Even if he got lucky and made it, he'd be right in Edward's line of fire, making it more difficult for his brother to attack. No, with things in such close quarters, it was best for him to just stay out of the way. Apparently, Alphonse wasn't alone in his thinking, for when he took another step back, he ran into Fletcher.

"Oh, sorry," Alphonse apologized automatically.

Fletcher stepped meekly aside.

"Sorry."

"It was my fault."

The boy who was posing as Alphonse Elric was quite small, shorter even than Edward. He was slender and, unlike his short-tempered brother, had a sweet, gentle look to him. Alphonse could well have been mad at him for stealing his identity, but the worried look in Fletcher's eyes as he watched his brother fight made Alphonse hold his tongue. He could see Fletcher didn't want to be here either.

Just then, Edward landed a lucky blow on Russell's shoulder with his stone sword.

Fletcher gasped.

"Look," Alphonse said, noticing his concern, "I'm sure your brother won't lose too badly—he does have a Stone, after all."

Fletcher said nothing until he was satisfied that his brother wasn't injured. He turned to Alphonse.

"Why aren't you pitching in, Alphonse? You can use alchemy too, can't you?"

"A little," Alphonse replied. "Nothing like my brother. How about you?"

If Russell could use alchemy and his younger brother was helping him with his research, it stood to reason that Fletcher would be able to perform at least a little alchemy. Fletcher seemed about to tell him something when Russell swung his sword directly at them.

"Whoa!"

In a blur of action, Alphonse grabbed Fletcher and dodged aside.

"Are you trying to hurt your own brother!?" Edward shouted at Russell.

Russell seemed flustered. "I-it's just hard to hold back when I'm using the Stone! Fletcher, are you okay!?"

"I-I'm okay, thanks to Alphonse," Fletcher said. "Thank you, Alphonse."

"You're welcome." Alphonse put Fletcher down, noticing the scars of battle on the surface of the courtyard.

Smashed cobblestones from Russell's attacks lay everywhere, perhaps due to his inexperience wielding the Stone. It had been a fierce competition. Edward's shoulders were heaving with the exertion of dodging Russell's attacks, and Russell's legs trembled with exhaustion.

Alphonse figured it was about time they called a retreat. His brother was far too mad to fight with a level head, and if he kept on like this he might get seriously injured.

"Ed! Let's go!"

"Huh!?"

Fletcher ran across the shattered stones to his brother. "That's enough, Russ!"

"What do you mean?" Russell scowled.

Neither brother was ready to listen to his sibling, but with both of the younger brothers trying to put an end to the fighting, the tension eased. The battle was drawing to a close.

"Ed, if you get hurt, we won't be able to get away. Let's pull out for tonight."

He pulled grumbling Edward towards the wall they had scaled. Back in the courtyard, Fletcher held Russell back from following them.

"If Mr. Mugear sees us, we'll get caught. That's enough for tonight."

Russell swore softly, but let Fletcher lead him away from the fight by the hand. Edward, being dragged off by his own brother, called out to him.

"Hey! How old are you? I'm fifteen!"

Russell shrugged at the unexpected question. "What's it matter? You're leaving. And don't come back!"

"Come on, Ed. Let's get out of here," Alphonse urged.

But Edward wasn't satisfied. "Wait! Tell me how old you are!"

Russell sneered. "Fifteen, same as you. Satisfied?"

Alphonse finally dragged Edward, wailing, outside. "One second you're raving mad, and now you're crying like a baby!" he complained.

Once over the wall, the two headed toward Belsio's house on the outskirts of town. They hadn't gotten into the laboratory, but they had avoided getting caught by the guards, and for the time being, they could rest. Edward stared straight ahead as they walked. Finally, he spoke.

"Hey, Alphonse . . ."

"What?"

"What do you think?"

"Well, he is using a trial Stone," Alphonse replied, reviewing the battle in his mind. "But he was still pretty good on his own. I think he knows a lot of alchemy."

"That's not what I meant." Edward shook his head sharply.

"Huh? What, then?"

"How old do you think he is!? You don't believe he's the same age as me, do you? If he is, then how come . . ."

"Huh?" Alphonse looked at his brother with confusion. He had thought Edward was concerned about the Stone.

Edward stared into space, clearly distraught. "He was taller than me . . ."

If he was pretending to be younger, fine, Edward could

live with that. But if they really were the same age, then how could he be a full head taller? It wasn't fair!

"Is he really fifteen?" Edward asked, half to himself. "If so, then why is he so much taller than me? Why!?"

After a pause, Alphonse sighed wearily. "I don't know. Maybe he drinks a lot of milk?"

MEANWHILE, Mr. Mugear had called the Elric impostors into the main hall of the mansion. The town might have been feeling the strain of hard times, but Mugear's hall looked anything but impoverished. To see the luxuriousness of the interior, one might wonder if Mugear really needed the money he borrowed from the townspeople for his research. The truth was, the loans were all part of his plan. Even if he managed to synthesize gold through alchemy, without the town's craftsmen, Xenotime would never regain its former glory. He needed the craftsmen to work the gold he made, so they would get more orders for goldware, so he could make more gold to fill them. The wealth that followed would be uncountable.

Mugear borrowed money from the townspeople not to fund his research, but to keep the craftsmen nearby. Without gold, they might leave for better opportunities elsewhere, but few would go until they got their hard-earned money back. They had to wait for Mugear's Stone.

"So you drove away some bandits, eh, Master Edward?"

Mugear strode up the hall stairs, his stocky profile cutting an imposing figure even from a distance. He had been eating well.

"It was no big deal. They'd gotten it into their heads to take a peek at our laboratory, but they ran with their tails between their legs. I'm just glad you're all right, sir."

"I accepted your suggestion to hide in the cellar. But given your power, I thought perhaps that wasn't really necessary. I did so want to see how a State Alchemist fights!"

Russell bowed elegantly. "Alas, I am not perfect. Even in such an easy skirmish as tonight's, there is always the chance that . . . Well, I couldn't bear it if any harm came to you, sir."

Mugear laughed. "Ah, yes. For if something happened to me, you wouldn't be able to continue your research!"

Russell smiled. "Guilty as charged, sir. But I am an alchemist, and what alchemist would not long, above all else, to create the Philosopher's Stone?"

"Yet you weren't able to create it with the research funding that the military provided you," Mugear pointed out, raising an eyebrow.

"If I made it with the military's help, the fruits of my labor would all go to the military. That's why I prefer to conduct my experiments in secret."

Mugear grinned. He seemed to share Russell's disdain for the military. "Then you have a friend in me. You may conduct all the research you desire in the sanctuary of my laboratory."

"Thank you, sir. And on the dawn of the day when our work is complete, I will present you with the Philosopher's Stone."

"I look forward to it. Now, I'm going to bed. I'd like to see some progress soon . . . "

"Certainly, sir. Good night." Russell watched Mugear ascend the stairs, then turned and walked out. The smile had already faded from his lips. Fletcher hung back. He looked worried.

"Don't look like that," Russell said as they left the mansion and headed toward the laboratory. "I handled it well. Act nervous, and he'll suspect something." He turned to his brother and smiled.

The worry faded from Fletcher's face. "But . . . the real State Alchemist was here tonight, Russ. How much longer can we keep our secret?"

"As long as we can keep those two away from Mugear. If we overreact or try to drive them out of town, we'll only raise suspicion. We'll just deal with them as the need arises. Luckily, Mugear doesn't suspect a thing. Come on, we've got research to do."

"You know what's going to happen if we get caught, don't you? Impersonating military personnel, conning the townspeople . . . We've even taken their money!"

Russell turned to face his brother. "Listen, to make the Philosopher's Stone, we need money and the right equipment.

We have that here now. We can't leave. We'll be done soon. We only have to keep up this act until then."

"How long have you been saying we're almost done? You know we can't do this by ourselves!"

Russell sighed. "You're right. We need more information. Be patient, just a little longer."

"Russell!"

"It's for the good of the town," Russell muttered. He walked back into the laboratory, leaving Fletcher alone in the hall.

"I don't want to lie anymore," he said softly. But there was no one to hear him.

Chapter Two

Silver Eyes

THE FOLLOWING MORNING, Edward opened his eyes to a view of the underside of the eaves of Belsio's house, located on the outskirts of town. The sun was already high in the sky, its light harsh to his bleary eyes. As he sat up, sand trickled down the sides of his face.

"Sleep outside in a place like this and you're bound to wake up with sand in your hair." Belsio's voice emanated from the front of the house. He was seated working on a tool of some kind. Next to him, Alphonse was oiling the wheels of a mining cart.

"Morning, Ed. You've got little sand-cakes on your cheeks."

Edward groaned and brushed the sand off his face. His head was pounding from the beating it had taken the night before.

Belsio laughed. "I said you could sleep in the house, but you wouldn't listen."

"If people in town heard you'd taken us in, what would they say?"

"Don't know. I was just in town, and no one seemed to care."

Edward gave him a puzzled look.

"Never mind," Belsio continued, waving his hand dismissively. "Your brother fetched some water in that basin over there. Go wash yourself off. Take care to clean your eyes out good. A lot of folks in town don't see too well anymore on account of all the sand."

Edward thanked him, stood up, and dusted himself off. "A wash sounds good right about now." He located the oil drum filled with water toward the back of the house.

Edward patted his growling stomach. "I could go for a bite to eat, too!" He considered Lemac's tavern, but the chances of getting thrown out seemed pretty high. "We missed dinner last night . . ."

Edward's stomach growled as he brushed the sand off his body. A sudden sharp pain made him stop abruptly. Lifting his shirt, he discovered he was covered with black and blue welts. He hadn't noticed them before, but now that he had, he realized he was aching all over. "That jerk didn't hold back, did he?"

Of course, neither had Edward—but knowing that the impostor must be hurting just as much as he did little to ease Edward's pain. The things that guy had said! He had really tried to get under Edward's skin. And it made Edward even madder that he had succeeded and made him lose his cool. Not to mention that, even though they were the same age, the impostor was at least a head taller.

"He was lying about his age! I know it!" Edward insisted, sounding more hopeful than confident. "Let's see . . . I grow about two inches a year . . . And we were about eight inches apart . . . So . . . four years? That would make him *nineteen!*" Edward proclaimed, heedless of the possibility that he might not grow two inches next year. Somewhere along the way he had progressed from estimating Russell's age to imagining himself at age nineteen: tall, handsome . . .

"Nineteen!" Edward crowed, turning to Alphonse with a big grin.

"Um, Ed? What's up? You're kind of smirking . . ."

"Huh? N-nothing." Edward let his hair fall over his face to hide his expression. He wanted to give a little thumbs up and shout, *Me at nineteen! Eat your heart out!* But Alphonse would just frown at him, and that would be the end of that.

Edward turned around to find himself eye-to-eye with Elisa, the girl from the day before.

"Hey! It's the bandit brothers!"

"Oh, hi. You're Lemac's daughter, right?"

"Yep. I'm Elisa!"

She smiled as though she'd completely forgotten yesterday's events.

"Elisa's just come up from town," Belsio said. "She tells me Lemac invited you down for lunch."

"Thanks, but I don't care to be called a liar again."

"You're still pretending to be the Elric brothers?" Elisa put her hands on her hips and pouted. "Lying is *wrong*, you know!"

"We're not lying!"

"Papa says you want to get into the alchemy lab real bad. He says it's funny. He says you must really be excited about alchemy to go that far!"

Edward laughed bitterly. Apparently there was no use trying to convince Elisa of the truth. "Well, why not. We have to eat."

"Okay, but no more lying!" Elisa ran off after Belsio.

"You're not coming back with us, Elisa?" Alphonse called out behind her. She showed no sign of slowing down.

"I'm helping Mr. Belsio today!" she shouted back over her shoulder.

The two watched Elisa and Belsio head off toward his garden before turning and setting out for town.

Along the way, the people they passed shot them glances and laughed. A few even warned them to knock off the tomfoolery and cut the crap. Apparently, word of their humiliation had reached town. Still, at least they weren't being treated like outlaws. Everyone seemed to have just written them off as mischievous kids. When they reached town, Alphonse went off to have a look around while Edward headed for the tavern.

Yesterday a newcomer, today a laughingstock.

Edward plodded into Lemac's place with a scowl on his face.

"There you are. Hungry?" Lemac greeted him with a look of great condescension, but cheerfully went in back to prepare him breakfast.

"So," called Lemac from the kitchen. "I hear you tried to sneak into Mr. Mugear's place last night."

He doesn't waste any time, does he?

"Yeah, that's right. How'd you know?"

Lemac laughed. "You must have really been itching to see that lab. Posing as alchemists, raiding the Mugear mansion . . . I've got to admit, I'm impressed!"

Edward sighed. The misunderstandings were running so deep, it didn't seem worth defending himself anymore.

"You've got a lot of determination for a kid, but you really ought to think about directing your energy in a more positive direction. If you want to become a great alchemist, why don't you try to join the State Alchemists, like Master Edward?"

"'Like Master Edward' . . . " Edward muttered. *Why hasn't anyone ever called* me *"master"?*

"People figure all the talk about the Philosopher's Stone went to your head."

"True enough."

"So why don't you just give up your little act and be

straight with us? Tell us your real name."

Edward lacked the will to shout *I told you my real name!*
At the same time, he didn't want to take the easy way out
and make something up.

"Edward," he said quietly. "And my brother is Alphonse.
It's the truth."

Lemac frowned. He seemed deep in thought.

"It's true!" Edward insisted.

Lemac took on a look of resignation as he filled Edward's
coffee cup. "I guess sometimes people have the same names."
Apparently he was finally willing to give the brothers the
benefit of the doubt. Or, perhaps, half the benefit of the doubt.
"Still, to keep from confusing you with Master Edward and
his brother, I'll just call you Ed and Al, okay?"

"Fine."

"And no more playing at bandits!"

Edward's heart sank in his chest. Still, this was better than
being called a liar and getting tossed out on the street. He
decided the time had come for him to keep his head down
and focus on finding out everything he could about this so-
called "Stone."

"So everyone's convinced they'll be able to create a real
Philosopher's Stone?"

Lemac shrugged and began drying cups. "Some things
you just have to believe in order to keep going, you know?"

Edward knew what he meant so well it hurt. There was no

guarantee that the Stone would get his brother's body back, but he couldn't give up hope. "Isn't it hard living here in the meantime?" Edward asked.

"Sure, it's hard. Some people leave. But a lot of us want a chance to use our skills again to work gold."

"But if you have enough money to loan some to Mugear, couldn't you use it to move and find a mine somewhere else?"

"Well, we couldn't just do that. Mr. Mugear's helped us out so much."

"But he bought all the rights to the mine, didn't he? And that killed off all the crops . . . "

Lemac said nothing.

"Isn't that Mugear's fault?"

Lemac sighed and sat down across from Edward. "Some might say that, but that's not the way it is to my mind. At least, it's not all Mr. Mugear's fault. Sure, we all meant to buy the rights to the mine together, but, truth be told, we were short on cash. And we were reluctant to sell our farmland to come up with the money. So Mr. Mugear put up his own money to make the purchase. And yes, some of the fields near the mine went bad from the dust, but everyone's lives improved. Some people might regret losing our green fields and orchards, but most of us were happy enough with the wealth we got in return. And once one person made it, everyone else wanted to get in on the act. That's why we all learned goldsmithing so fast. Now, none of us can forget those golden days. That's why we stay. For the love of gold."

Lost in memories, Lemac's eyes took on a faraway look. Edward wondered whether he was picturing the days of the gold rush or the green fields from before. One thing was clear: the town and the townspeople lacked their former spirit.

"Sounds like you're living in the past."

To his surprise, Lemac nodded in agreement. "We all have doubts somewhere in our hearts. But none of us who touched gold can forget what it was like—Mr. Mugear least of all. We want that glory back. We can't change our ways."

"Not even you, Mr. Lemac?"

"I guess not. Now that I've lived a life of luxury, I can't help but want that for Elisa. And I need to take care of my wife. She's in a hospital off in the countryside."

"Your wife?"

"Yeah. You think I could have built up a business like this with my rotten cooking? I'm here because I have to be, but this was my wife's place. The dust from the mines got to her, though, and she had to leave. Me, I'm just carrying on until I can find some other way to make a living. It's a darn shame, really." He seemed resigned to his fate.

A town caught tight in the chains of its past. Chains of gold . . .

Edward sighed and paid for his meal.

WHILE EDWARD WAS TALKING with Lemac, Alphonse was making his way to the town's pharmacy in hopes of finding some bandages and liniment for Edward's bruises. The townspeople laughed when they saw him, but he was grateful they weren't hostile.

"Hello!" he said, ducking into the pharmacy. An older woman peered out at him from between bottles lined up on a shelf.

"Ah, one of those kids everyone's been talking about. You've sure been causing a ruckus."

What a greeting, thought Alphonse, but he couldn't bring himself to defend having trespassed at the mansion. He decided to let the matter drop. He was a customer here, after all.

"Do you have anything that's good for, um, bruises?"

"I've just the thing," the woman said, perking up. "Let me mix you up a batch." She pointed to a chair in the corner. "Have a seat over there—if you can sit in that armor of yours."

"I'll just stand, thanks. Don't mind me."

Alphonse stood patiently in the middle of the pharmacy while the lady brought various bottles into a back room to formulate a salve. Suddenly, the door to the pharmacy opened.

"Hello?"

It was Fletcher. When he saw Alphonse standing next

to the entrance, he stopped dead in his tracks. *He looks nervous,* Alphonse thought. *Understandably! He's stolen my name, and the last time we met, our brothers were trying to kill each other!*

The pharmacist hadn't noticed her latest customer yet.

He's probably scared I'm going to reveal he's a fraud . . . or maybe he thinks I already have.

After standing in silence for a few moments, Fletcher quietly turned and began to walk out of the store. But then the pharmacist caught sight of him.

"Oh, Master Alphonse! Did you need something?"

"Um . . . " Fletcher's voice trembled, even though the pharmacist's greeting must have assured him that his disguise hadn't been uncovered.

Uncovered or not, your guilty conscience won't let you rest, will it? Still, Alphonse didn't resent the boy for not confessing. In fact, he almost sympathized with him because he seemed so obviously guilt ridden.

The pharmacist stood smiling at them, utterly unaware of what was running through the two boys' heads. "Master Alphonse, please don't be angry at these boys. They only pretended to be you because they idolize Master Edward's talent so."

She thinks he's nervous because I'm "pretending" to be him!

"Don't worry, we've told them not to bother you anymore.

Now, what can I get you, Master Alphonse?"

Fletcher appeared on the verge of tears. He hesitated between Alphonse and the pharmacist, unable to decide what to do or say.

"Uh, um . . . I came for some medicine," he managed to squeeze out at last. "Something for bruises. My brother bumped himself . . . " His voice trailed off until it was barely a whisper.

"So!" the pharmacist exclaimed, glaring at Alphonse. "Was that salve you wanted for treating bruises your brother incurred from fighting Master Edward last night, by any chance?"

Alphonse gulped. Her eyes burned into him . . . but at least she was still mixing the salve. She'd probably sell it to him regardless of his answer, but not without scolding him first, just like his brother always did.

Before she could continue, Fletcher took a step forward. "Um, actually, my brother's bruise wasn't from fighting. He just fell down. It has nothing to do with the two, um, impostors."

"Well, that stands to reason," the pharmacist said. "I didn't think a small boy like that could hurt your brother." She handed a bottle to Alphonse. "There you go. Thanks for waiting. Soak a bandage in that and put it on the bruise. And tell your brother to behave himself! Master Edward is the forgiving sort, and the townspeople have laughed this whole affair off as a silly kid's prank for now, but if you don't stay out of trouble . . ."

Alphonse took the bottle and nodded his thanks.

The pharmacist picked up another bottle and gave it to Fletcher. "And here's Master Edward's salve and some powdered syrup to drink. Just dissolve it in warm water. No, no . . . there's no need to pay."

"That's all right, I'll pay. Thank you, ma'am." Fletcher paid the full amount against the pharmacist's protests and walked out into the street beside Alphonse.

Several paces from the pharmacy, Fletcher stopped abruptly. "I'm sorry," he said, in a voice so full of pain that Alphonse stopped short. Fletcher's shoulders were trembling.

"If you're so sorry, why don't you just tell them the truth?" *Wouldn't it be better to just get it off his chest?*

"I'm sorry. I never dreamed you two would come here, to this town. I'm sorry the townspeople got mad at you because of us."

"So you never thought about what would happen if you ran into the real Elric brothers, huh?"

Fletcher nodded sadly. "I know what we're doing isn't right."

"But you're still doing it anyway! That makes it even worse!"

"I know. I'm sorry."

Alphonse could tell from watching Fletcher now and last night that living a lie was hard for him. His older brother, Russell, had a face that revealed little, and he had been so busy picking on Edward that he had given no indication of his feelings on the matter, but Fletcher was different. Every move he made revealed his inner turmoil.

"You disagree with your brother, don't you?"

Fletcher sighed, unable to answer. He was tired of all the lying.

"If you can apologize to me, why can't you just tell your brother how you feel? It's cowardly not to confront him."

"I know it is, but . . ." Fletcher's head drooped. "If *I* turn against him, he won't have anyone. He'll be all alone."

Alphonse didn't know what to say.

"There'll be no one left on his side! I mean, it's probably our fault because of all the lies, but we're on our own. What would he do if I left him here?"

"He could leave *with* you!"

Fletcher shook his head. "If that was all it took, I would have confronted him before all the lying started." A black spot appeared on the ground at the boy's feet. A tear, quickly swallowed by the dusty soil. "I can't leave—not by myself. I have to stick by my brother." Fletcher wiped the tears from his eyes with the back of his hand. "I can't believe I'm telling you this. You're the victim here, and I'm the one who's crying. I must be nuts."

"If I felt all on my own, living a lie every day, I'd lose it too." Alphonse didn't think Fletcher deserved his sympathy, but it was hard to be cold to him. "I know how you feel," Alphonse said kindly. "I'm a younger brother too. I know you feel like you've got to do what he says, be loyal, and not question him. But there are some things in life that are more important than that."

Alphonse put his hand on Fletcher's shoulder. "If you two are all alone in the world, that means if your brother's doing something wrong, you're the only one who can stop him— even if you have to fight with him. If you don't, who will? If you can't pull him back by yourself, then you'll have to ask for help, but somehow, you've got to stop him before he goes too far! You can't just hope this will blow over by itself, and you can't rely on someone else to take care of it for you."

Fletcher remained silent.

"That's just my opinion, of course," mumbled Alphonse, suddenly self-conscious. He knew he was right, but he was afraid he had been too harsh.

Fletcher stared at the ground for a while, then raised his eyes to Alphonse. "You must get along well with your brother."

Fletcher's face seemed a little brighter than before, underneath the streaks his tears had left on his cheeks. Although he hadn't really acknowledged Alphonse's words, Alphonse was glad that Fletcher had cheered up a little at least. A few minutes ago, Alphonse thought he was going to collapse on the spot.

"We get along all right, but that doesn't mean we don't fight," Alphonse told him, trying to sound encouraging.

"Really? Actually, my brother and I haven't fought in a while. You know, he didn't tell Mr. Mugear that he lost to your brother last night. He tries to act all cool, but really he's a sore loser. He'd never tell anyone if he got hurt in a fight or had trouble with his research. He pretends he doesn't care. But I've seen his face when he thinks no one is watching. That's why I've got to buy his medicine for him."

The boys caught each other's eye and laughed. Fletcher pulled one of the packets of powdered syrup out of his bag and handed it to Alphonse. "This is supposed to be good to drink when you use the salve. It really works." He placed the packet in Alphonse's hand.

"I can't . . . " Alphonse began.

"It's a fair trade . . . "

Leaving Alphonse to ponder his words, Fletcher turned and walked away down the street.

"WHAT'S *that* supposed to mean? His syrup is supposed to pay for using our identities?" Edward waved the packet of powder under his brother's nose. They were standing outside Lemac's tavern.

"Stop waving that around! You'll spill it!" Alphonse snapped. He got to work applying the bottle of salve to the cloth bandages Lemac had been kind enough to give them. "I don't think that's what he meant by 'fair trade.' If he did, I wouldn't have taken the medicine."

"Then what *did* he mean?"

"Um . . . I'm not sure."

Edward hadn't been there. How could he explain it to him? They sat down on the bench next to the entrance.

"You're too nice sometimes, Al. You should have just told the truth, right there in front of the pharmacist. That Fletcher kid needs a good sock in the jaw to straighten him out. I can't believe he goes around pretending to be you and all he has to say for himself is 'sorry.'"

Edward was snippy, probably because of the sting of the bruises Russell had given him.

Alphonse just shrugged. "She wouldn't believe me even if I told her we were the real thing. I mean, *they* look more like us than *we* do!"

"Huh? What do you mean by that? Just because Russell's more even-tempered, and smarter, and cooler, and tall—*ow!*" Edward yelped as Alphonse slapped a wet bandage on his banged-up leg. "Look," Edward continued, "I'm sure they've got their reasons, but so do we. Let's focus on how we're going to get what we want."

"All right."

They had come for one thing: the Philosopher's Stone. Or, failing that, information that might lead them to the means of making one themselves.

"Well, at least we're officially 'bandits' now," muttered Edward. In other words, he was planning to raid the Mugear mansion again. "In any case, I need more info, so we'll have to stick around town a while longer."

"You need to rest up, too. And you might as well take that medicine I got." Alphonse applied more bandages.

Edward looked at him suspiciously. "You really think this stuff works?" he asked, holding the packet up to the light to inspect its contents.

"I'm going to go help Belsio. It's the least I can do after he took us in. Drink that, okay?" Alphonse scooped up the empty bottle of salve, stood up, and headed off toward the outskirts of town.

Edward sat with the packet of powder in his hand. "What if it makes me all numb or something?" he muttered to himself, frowning.

The truth was, he just didn't like to take medicine.

THE AIR IN TOWN had been clear that morning, but by evening, the haze of dust blocked visibility beyond a few yards. Belsio stood watching the dust trickle up in streams like smoke off the mounds of rubble near the mine. He turned to Elisa and Alphonse behind him.

"Elisa? Al? That's enough for today. The wind's picking up."

Elisa looked up from where she was diligently clearing rocks, her little hands wrapped tightly in tiny work gloves to protect them from the rough stones. Alphonse was putting up boards to support a half-completed stone fence.

It would be a while before they finished the wall and it could finally serve its purpose to protect the waterway that led to Belsio's field. Even the sections that had been completed not too long ago were already getting worn down by the constant barrage of windblown sand. Those sections had to be shored up, and they had to finish the wall around the reservoir and field as well. It was harder than Alphonse had expected to work out here in the sand. But Belsio had done so much already, and he had done it all by himself.

"Once we finish this, you can make the field bigger. I bet having more greenery here will brighten up the whole town," Alphonse said. Perhaps he was being a hopeless optimist, but in his heart he felt it was true.

"I think so too," Elisa said, her eyes sparkling. "Won't everyone be surprised when they see it? It'll remind them of how beautiful our town used to be."

It was just a touch of green in a brown, barren wasteland. But if it spread, how the hearts of the townspeople would soar! Elisa had never known anything but this arid landscape herself, but when she saw the first tree that Belsio had planted, it brought tears to her eyes. That was when she started coming every day to help him.

"I was so surprised," she told Alphonse. "It was so big and green! When I told my Papa, he said the whole town used to be like that!"

Alphonse recalled his own hometown. There had been a lot of rock and sand there too, but at least a little vegetation as well. He had been shocked when he arrived in Xenotime. Compared to the places he knew, this was a desert. "I hope the town becomes green again, Mr. Belsio."

"I hope so too."

"We'll make it happen, Mr. Belsio! I'll help out until it's done," Elisa piped up. "Promise?"

Belsio nodded. "Promise."

With just one man and a little girl, who knew how long it would take?

"I'll take you back home," Belsio told Elisa at last.

Elisa jumped up and surveyed the vegetable garden. "We picked some good vegetables today, didn't we, Mr. Belsio?"

"The ripest I've seen," Belsio assured her. The basket beside him held three bright red tomatoes. "Thanks to your help, Elisa."

Elisa giggled. Even Belsio's stern face softened into a smile. "Come on, let's go." Belsio picked the basket up in one hand, and the three walked down towards the town, which was already shrouded in a brown twilight haze.

WHEN THEY ARRIVED at Lemac's tavern, they found many of the townspeople gathered inside. Edward and Lemac stood near the back, leaning on the counter.

"I'm home!"

Lemac, head drooping, hands folded in front of him, looked up at the sound of his daughter's voice. A warmth rose to his face. "Welcome back, Elisa."

Elisa ran to give her father her usual greeting hug, then stopped in her tracks. She was used to everyone greeting her when she came into the tavern, but tonight, no one had said a word.

"Papa, is something wrong?"

"Well . . . no." Lemac fell silent.

Alphonse looked at his brother. "What's going on?"

"They've just been discussing the town's progress . . . or lack thereof," he answered, looking glumly around the room. Edward picked up a coffee pot and refilled his own cup. He seemed happy to be in the role of a detached observer.

"Papa, what happened?" Elisa asked, looking from face to face. Belsio handed her the tomatoes from the basket.

"Elisa, could you wash these for me? Be gentle, now."

Elisa nodded and took the basket back to the well behind the tavern.

"Thanks, friend," Lemac said softly.

"Don't mention it. Now what's going on?"

Belsio sat down next to Lemac and surveyed the silent crowd. Without exception, the faces were carved with deep lines of worry. They looked beaten and worn out.

"Norris left," Lemac said bitterly.

Belsio seemed surprised. "Really?"

"Yeah. He gave everyone the news at noon. He's already gone. His son's not doing too well, he said."

Norris was one of the most skillful goldsmiths in town. He had been an outspoken supporter of Mugear's research to develop the Philosopher's Stone and was the biggest contributor by far. But his two-year-old son had been bedridden since the beginning of the year. The dust had gotten to his lungs.

"I see," Belsio said. "Sounds like he didn't have much choice." Belsio and Norris had often found themselves on the opposite side of debates, with Belsio strongly urging the townspeople to give up their goldsmithing and Norris striving to rouse support for Mugear's efforts to manufacture the Stone. But they had known each other for a long time, and Belsio was sad to hear he had left. "He was a great goldsmith."

"Aye, one of the best. Master Mugear was sorry to hear he'd left, too," Lemac added bitterly. "Of course, that was after we told him the funding for his research would go down now that Norris is gone."

"I see," Belsio said. Now the sour faces in the room made even more sense.

When he heard that Norris had left, Mugear came to town and told everyone that it would be difficult to continue the research without their biggest supporter. The town was in a bind. With everyone in such dire straits already, they had nothing left to give. On the other hand, if they stopped funding Mugear's research, not only would they never get their Philosopher's Stone, but all the money they had contributed so far would go down the drain.

"Even if we keep supporting him, there's no guarantee he'll ever manage to make the Stone! So why don't we cut our losses now?" demanded one of the townsfolk.

"What about all the money we've spent so far?" asked another. "I have faith he'll succeed!"

"Fine! If you believe in him, give him your money!"

"But that means the rest of us will have to give more!"

"Don't you want to get this town back on its feet? We were the best goldsmiths anywhere! Are we just going to let our gift die with us?"

"All I'm saying is we can't live out here in this wasteland on dreams alone!"

Heated exchanges continued to reverberate throughout the tavern. This was only the latest in a series of such scenes. But it seemed the months of pent-up frustration had finally reached the boiling point. The shouting got louder and louder, and no one listened to what anyone else was saying.

"We're just doing Mugear's bidding! What's in it for us?"

"We should have bought the rights to the mine while we still could . . ."

"Hey, you were just as blinded by the gold as I was!"

"Oh, yeah!?"

"Quiet down, everyone!" Lemac ran out into the middle of the room, waving down the people who were jumping up from their chairs. "Fighting amongst ourselves will only make matters worse!"

"So what do you suggest we do, then?" someone challenged.

Lemac had no answer. He understood both sides—those who wanted to give more money and those who wanted to find another way—and he was torn.

Someone in the crowd piped up, "Hey, Ed . . . Al . . . You went to the lab, didn't you? Well? Did they have the Stone? Are they making any progress?" All eyes turned to Alphonse and Edward.

"Um . . ." Alphonse stalled, unsure of what to say. "We, uh, didn't exactly get inside. They chased us off."

Edward, seated beside him, calmly sipped his coffee. Alphonse realized that his brother wasn't paying attention to anything going on inside the tavern. He was gazing out the window at something outside . . . golden hair, waving in the breeze.

"Maybe we should ask Master Edward how they're coming along?"

"You think he'd tell us? It's top-secret research . . ."

Some of the townspeople cradled their heads in their hands. They'd been running on hope too long. Now it was time for the truth.

Then Elisa came back into the tavern, her voice a ray of light in the gloom that filled the room. "Look! Aren't they beautiful?" She held the tomatoes, still glistening wet, in her hand. They were a vibrant red. "These tomatoes are almost as pretty as goldware, don't you think, Papa?" Elisa held the tomatoes up high for everyone to see. "I planted the seeds these grew from myself! I thought maybe nobody had seen one of these before, so I brought 'em here to show you!" She wanted to share what she had felt when she first saw the tomatoes shining red in Belsio's vegetable patch. "Belsio keeps saying he wishes we had a lot more of these around, so we're growing 'em!" Elisa smiled innocently. "I wonder how long it would take for everyone to grow these!"

Nobody said a word.

Edward was the one to finally break the silence. "Ha! From the mouths of babes . . ." He set down his coffee cup and picked up one of Elisa's tomatoes. "It's got good color."

"Really?"

"Yep!" He handed the tomato back to Elisa with a smile. "But I think it'll be a while before anyone else can grow one of these in their yards."

"Ed . . ." Alphonse began worriedly. There was no point dashing the child's hopes. But Elisa smiled.

"That's okay! We've still got lots of rocks to move, and then *everyone* can grow green things. They might be a little scraggly and yellow at first, but soon there'll be green plants everywhere! They change color every day, you know. All we hafta do is move all those rocks!"

Just move rocks—it seemed so simple when she said it. Never mind that it would take years, or that the sandy soil might not be able to support any plants. Elisa's words touched the heart of everyone sitting in the tavern.

"She's right. If we just clear the land . . . "

"Well, Belsio? What do you think? Could we get back some of the green we've lost?"

Belsio frowned. "It won't be easy." The tavern was silent. "It would take years," he continued. "And it might not work out in the end. Besides, we'd never be as rich as we were when we were goldsmiths."

"True. We're better off counting on Mugear's research!"

"And digging for that gold mine . . . "

"We can't go back to farming now!"

Edward scowled. "Yeah. Why don't you just keep on clinging to your dreams of gold, all of you!" His voice was cold. All eyes turned to him, but he was unfazed. "You know that synthesizing gold through alchemy is illegal, don't you?"

" . . . We know."

"So what are you going to do if you get caught? Maybe you're thinking because you used to be a gold-mining town, you can produce a little and no one will notice? Or you're hoping you'll find that new gold vein before word gets out?" Edward's words cut deeply. He was provoking the crowd, but there was nothing they could say. "You're looking for a gold vein that you might never find, throwing money at a Stone that might never get made, giving up your health . . . But you still refuse to look for another way to live your lives?"

Lemac spoke softly on behalf of the silent crowd. "You're young, Ed. You can do anything you want. But we're too old to start over. We don't know if we can make it somewhere else. And we have a trade we want to pass on to our children . . ."

"Fine," Edward snorted. "Then stay here and wait forever. I don't care."

"Well, we know that won't do, but we're not sure what to do next. No one can agree on a direction—"

Edward interrupted Lemac's rationalizations. "Maybe you can't agree on anything because you haven't even chosen the path you're on now! When will the money you've donated to Mugear's research bear fruit? When will you get your money back a hundredfold? This is Mugear's trap, and you're stuck in it!"

"You don't understand. You have your life ahead of you, but we have our past behind us. Once you've lived as richly as we have, you can't settle for less."

"Maybe you're right," Edward said sarcastically. He stood up, walked to the door and opened it to leave—then stopped to address the crowd in the tavern. "Call me crazy, but I could never depend on someone else for my livelihood. I couldn't live like that."

Edward closed the door and walked out into the street before turning around. "And you—why don't you say something?" he growled at Russell, who was standing by the door. "You know I don't like you much either."

"I couldn't care less what you think of me."

Edward chuckled mischievously. "How about the towns-people? Do you care what they think? Here's an idea. Why don't you go in there and tell them you need more cash for your research. Tell them how much you've spent on it so far. See what they think of you then."

Russell grimaced. "It's . . . for the town."

"'For the town'?"

"You're just causing trouble here. Why don't you leave?"

"Me? I'd say it's *you* who's causing the trouble!" Edward retorted. "Say what you will, we're not going anywhere. In fact, I think we'll settle in for an extended stay. Sorry, pal." Edward slapped Russell on the shoulder and sauntered off down the street.

Alphonse quickly caught up to his brother. He glanced back and saw Russell still standing in the street. He hadn't made a move to open the tavern door.

AT TWO IN THE MORNING, a few hours later than the night before, Edward and Alphonse were back at the wall of the Mugear mansion.

"He won't be expecting us to come back so soon. I told him we'd be in town for a while," whispered Edward.

"I hope Russell and Fletcher are asleep."

Using the same maneuver as the night before, they scaled the wall.

"After that fight last night and the trip into town, he's got to be asleep by now."

"Speaking of which, we've been through the exact same things. Shouldn't we be asleep?"

"Hey, I'm tired too. Just hang in there a little longer."

They dropped down inside the wall and made straight for the laboratory. The mansion grounds were quiet. They saw no sign of the impostors anywhere.

Edward pressed his ear to the laboratory door. "Doesn't sound like anyone's home."

"How are we going to open it? If we make a passageway, the noise and light of the alchemy will give us away!" Alphonse glanced around nervously.

Edward laughed. "With this!" He held out a small key.

"Where did you—?" Alphonse began.

"I took it from Russell's pocket when we ran into him on the street today!"

Alphonse frowned. "You're getting worse, Ed . . . "

"Getting better, I'd say! Let's get this open!"

Edward slid in the key and quietly opened the door. They were in.

There was no one inside. A great number of beakers and flasks lined the wall, and a container filled with steam was positioned before a large furnace. The container held a row of flasks filled with some liquid. They were being maintained at a constant temperature.

"Hmm . . . " Edward scanned the room. "With a setup like

this, you can afford to not watch your samples every minute of the day. I can see why they needed all that money."

Edward passed his eyes over the stacks of books and papers covered with hastily scrawled notes. Alphonse began looking through the documentation while keeping an eye on the door in case someone should pay them a visit. The two possessed a knowledge of alchemy far surpassing any layperson, so they would be able to gauge the progress of the research simply by scanning the notes and experiments in progress.

"It looks like they're on the right track, all right," Edward remarked, putting down one sheaf of files as he looked for the next. Scattered throughout the workplace were strange lumps of materials discarded halfway through some alchemical process, rocks that glowed with a dull light, and pots of various sizes filled with a variety of colored liquids. The mess was testimony to just how seriously Russell was pursuing his research.

He talks like a lightweight, but he knows a fair bit about alchemy, Edward noted. Then he saw something that made him groan. He showed the notebook he had been leafing through to Alphonse. "Look at this, Al. Talk about extreme methods!"

The notebook described in detail a very forceful and dangerous method for making a Stone. The results of the experiment hadn't been recorded, but from the bloodstains covering the bottom half of the notebook, Edward had a pretty good idea what happened.

"Fletcher must have it rough, trying to look after a brother like that," Alphonse said sympathetically. When they had met at the pharmacy, Fletcher had mentioned that he was often sent there to obtain medicine. Apparently, Russell got injured a lot—and not just in fights.

"He's in a real hurry." Edward gazed at a broken rack for storing chemicals, left where it had splintered apart. "They don't even take the time to clean up." He took another long look around the room. "It seems like they're on the verge of a breakthrough—this must be their sprint to the finish. But they can't figure out the final step, so they're trying every experiment in the book . . . But you know . . . something's odd about all this."

Alphonse held his tongue. He could see Edward was lost in thought and knew better than to disturb him.

"Yeah, there's definitely something strange going on here. You know, it's almost as if . . . "

Muttering on, Edward searched through the file closest to him, then dropped it and picked up the next closest one. Edward had unusual powers of concentration. It was this focus that had earned him the title of State Alchemist at the age of twelve. He had good research instincts, as well.

Alphonse stood by, watching Edward quietly, until he noticed something odd out of the corner of his eye. At first he thought it was a shadow cast by his brother as he moved about the room, but when he looked more closely, he realized it was something altogether different.

"Ed!"

"Huh? What is it?"

It was times like this when Alphonse appreciated his older brother the most. No matter how focused, no matter how dire the circumstances, Edward always gave Alphonse his due. In fact, it was precisely during tense moments like this that he was least likely to shush him or resent an interruption. Sure, he might have snapped at him once or twice a long time ago, when they were still kids, but these days he would never do that. No matter what was going on, Edward always heeded Alphonse's impressions and opinions—even when the last thing Edward wanted was an interruption.

Alphonse had asked him why he was so obliging once, and Edward had told him simply, "'Cause you're my partner." Alphonse had never been so surprised or pleased as when he heard those words on a day not long after Edward had become a State Alchemist. Alphonse knew his older brother's profession was a serious affair, and all he could do was follow along and try not to get in the way. He felt guilty, that he should be doing more himself, but he couldn't think what. When his older brother said those words, he finally realized what he could do. He could support his brother as his brother supported him—as an equal.

That day the brothers decided that whatever trials awaited them, they would face them together. They would fight side by side. That day, Alphonse truly became Edward's partner.

Alphonse pointed at the wall behind Edward. "Doesn't that seem strange to you?"

Edward turned to look. "What? This wall?"

The wall didn't appear unusual. It was composed of sandy mortar and was completely nondescript. Edward carefully scanned the surface.

"The color. Isn't it a little different from the other walls? Or am I just seeing things?" Alphonse studied the surface intently, trying to determine what had caught his attention.

"Aha!" the brothers exclaimed simultaneously.

A thin line stood out on the wall's surface, barely wider than a hair. Upon closer inspection, they found two parallel lines about an arm's width apart, both stretching up close to the ceiling. The lines were so thin they would most likely be invisible, but for a wan reddish light that seeped through them, giving a blush of color to the white surface of the wall.

"There's a room on the other side!" Edward exclaimed. The two exchanged glances, then began to push on the wall. They could feel its weight against their hands.

Noiselessly, the wall tilted inward, creating an entryway into the room beyond.

It was a small room, barely large enough to conduct

research in. It was rectangular and lacked even a single window. A lone desk stood in the very center, upon which a candle still flickered, as though someone had been there only a moment before.

And there, on the table, a single glass flask caught their gaze and held it fast. At the bottom of the corked vessel was a tiny amount of liquid.

A red liquid.

"Ed, you don't think . . . ?"

"I do. The Crimson Water." Edward was transfixed.

It wasn't the Philosopher's Stone, but it was far from a disappointment. In fact, it was the closest thing to the Stone they'd ever come across. They stood, transfixed.

The crimson color of the liquid seemed to move independently, dancing with every flicker of the candlelight. Though there were only a few drops, the reflected light filled the room, painting it as red as a cloud at sunset.

"Wow," murmured Edward.

The two had seen countless documents and failed attempts in their search for the Stone. Even the failures were often impressive, and sometimes, though the brothers strove to bridle their enthusiasm, the failures delighted them and gave them hope.

Like so many attempts they had observed, the Crimson Water was not a completed Philosopher's Stone. It wasn't even a Stone, for that matter. However, it promised something almost as valuable: a means to make the real Stone—or at least the best clue they had ever found.

The much-coveted Stone was a legend, almost a fable, and as such, there was little verifiable information to be had about it. It was said to possess a reddish light, the power to fascinate, and . . . unlimited alchemical potential.

The room shifted like the surface of a pool suffused with a scarlet glow.

Never had they seen something so enchanting, something with such presence, something they *wanted* so much.

"Al . . . I think we found it," Edward breathed, staring fixedly into the liquid. He could barely restrain the tremor of excitement in his voice. "This could advance our research by years. This might unravel the mystery of the Stone."

Although it was still just one step on the path, after years of nothing, it was a miracle. "There has to be some research data around here somewhere!" Edward slid his hands along the edge of the table. It was perfectly smooth. There were no drawers, nor was there anything else in the room: no shelves, no racks, nothing.

"Maybe they're in the other room?" Alphonse suggested.

"No, all the notes in that room seemed . . . odd, somehow." Edward crouched down to look under the bottom of the table. "I can't believe there's nothing here!" He walked along the walls of the room to make sure there weren't any more secret panels.

"Dammit!" Edward glared at the red fluid. "Just think if we had the recipe for this! We'd be so close!"

"Close . . . but not there. It's not the Stone, after all, is it?"

"It's not, but it's *something*, and it's very, very close."

Edward gently laid his finger on the flask, as if to touch the liquid through the glass. It felt cold, yet, at the same time, his hand felt hot. *Maybe it's just because I want it so much.*

"Of course, I've never seen it before, so I can't say this is it for sure, but Crimson Water is a pretty established element of alchemical lore about the Philosopher's Stone. No one's sure exactly what it has to do with the Stone, though. Is it some kind of by-product from making the Stone? Is it something derived from an entirely distinct alchemical process? Or does it harden and *become* the Stone? I've always thought it was something else, something different from the Stone, but it's definitely involved in the creation of the Stone, one way or another."

"I see," Alphonse said, nodding.

"So if that lump Russell carries around is a trial Stone, could this be a byproduct of its creation?"

"Wouldn't it be more important than that?" Alphonse asked. "Otherwise, why would they be hiding it in this secret room?"

"Good point. Maybe he made that trial lump out of this stuff."

"That seems like the most likely explanation to me."

"But if that's true, where are the records of this experiment? Even if it was a failure, they must have recorded their procedure somewhere."

"Maybe Russell carries his notes around with him. I mean, there are *bandits* in town, after all."

Edward shot a glance at his brother. "I'm surprised you'll admit it."

"What choice do we have, under the circumstances?"

"Well, yeah, but . . ." Edward began, suddenly self-conscious about the part he was playing in leading his younger brother off the straight and narrow path.

"Let's just get this over with before anyone has a chance to point fingers, okay?"

"Deal. And about those research notes," Edward continued, returning to the pressing matter at hand, "I don't think he carries them around with him."

"Why not?"

"Well, look at what's been left behind here . . . It's weird. It's like something vital is missing." Edward's eyes shone with the light of a sudden realization. "Their methods . . . They just don't make any sense!" He dashed back into the main laboratory and began shuffling through the piles of notes. "Look, here, here . . . and here!"

"Huh?"

"There's a huge gap in their research! They go from nothing to something with no steps in between! And there's not a scrap of evidence—no notes, no materials—to indicate they made any Crimson Water!"

"Huh? So that means—"

"Right! They *didn't* make it! They're researching *how* the Crimson Water was made! They're taking samples and trying to reverse-engineer the stuff!" Edward picked up scattered notes, scanned them, and tossed them aside. "But without the ingredients and procedure, their research is doomed."

"Is it that hard to figure out how something was made?"

"It's like splitting a hair into a hundred pieces—lengthwise. Much harder than creating something from scratch."

"So it's . . . impossible?"

"I'll say! It's like taking a sweater and trying to figure out how many strands of wool taken from what parts of which sheep were used to knit it."

"That sounds impossible, all right."

The brothers sighed in unison.

They knew it wouldn't be easy to find the Stone, and they knew better than to have gotten their hopes up, but this time . . . this time they had seemed so close! Their hearts sank to the floor, and a moment later shot through their throats when they heard a *third* sigh.

Russell stood in the doorway, arms folded, head hanging down. Fletcher was standing behind him.

"Y-you scared me to death!" Alphonse snapped.

"You could at least be a little noisier when you barge in like that!" Edward growled, humiliated that he had been sneaked up on twice in two nights. Russell's face was a serene mask.

"You're one to talk, breaking into a private residence in the middle of the night."

That was true enough. Edward winced under Russell's gaze.

Russell's face grew clouded. "You really think we've failed?"

Edward blinked. For a moment, he wasn't sure what Russell was talking about. Then he realized he was referring to their reverse-engineering experiment. He nodded.

"Your research? Yeah, it's dead in the water. When you start with a finished product like this, it's almost impossible to determine what went into making it."

Russell looked like he'd eaten something bitter. "I see. Well, you are the State Alchemist, after all." After a moment of silence, he added, "If that's what you think, it must be true."

Edward and Alphonse exchanged glances. Something had occurred to them both at the same time, and they didn't like it. "Wait a second," Edward said. "We didn't sneak in here without you knowing about it, did we? You knew I had the key!"

Russell smiled grimly. "You've got quite the reputation as a master alchemist, so I thought you'd know a few things I don't. I wanted a second opinion, you might say."

Edward shot a glance into the inner room. A scintillating crimson color spilled out of the opened wall into the room where they stood. "Look," he said, "alchemy is a science. You can't make something like that in there without the proper ingredients and methodology. Now that you've made us jump through your hoops to hear our opinion, I think I'm entitled to a question. What is that in there?"

"That? I call it the 'Water of Life.'"

"The 'Water of Life'? Is that the Crimson Water they say has something to do with creating the Philosopher's Stone?"

"Ah, yes. I've seen some documents that call it that. There are lots of theories about what it is, and just as many theories of how to make it." Russell picked up a book from the table near him and thumbed through it. "That wasn't made as part of the Philosopher's Stone project, though. It was made to be what it is—the Water of Life . . . though it's incomplete."

"Wait," Edward snapped, his temper igniting. "Aren't you getting paid to make the Philosopher's Stone? Isn't that why you're impersonating us!?"

His answer took Edward by surprise.

"I care nothing for the Philosopher's Stone . . . or gold, for that matter!"

"So you're just exploiting the townspeople!?" Edward shouted, boiling mad now.

Russell didn't flinch. "What I'm doing is still for the sake of the town. It's just that . . . I'm doing it in a slightly different way than I told them I would."

"So you're still deceiving them, you scumbag!"

Russell shrugged. "I didn't come here to win your praise."

Edward fumed. No matter what he said, Russell had a smooth comeback. Russell was always looking down on him, and this infuriated Edward. "You, you . . . I can't stand people like you!"

"Then why don't you leave? Go! You're putting us in jeopardy as it is."

"That's *your* problem!"

"If Mugear suspects anything, we'll be in big trouble."

Edward grinned. "Maybe I'll just go tell him then!"

Russell shook his head and sighed. "You just don't listen, do you? Maybe you'll listen to a little *pain*, hmm?"

Fletcher's worried voice came from behind him.

"Russell . . ." He tried to grab his big brother's arm, but Russell shook him off.

"Fletcher! Make sure Mugear stays in the cellar!"

"But . . ."

"Go!"

"What a great brother you are," muttered Alphonse, glaring at Russell. Fletcher looked as if he might say something. Then, without a word, he turned and left.

"We told Mugear to stay downstairs because of the *bandits*, but that doesn't change matters much. As long as you're around, we're in danger. So get out and don't come back!"

"If you want us to leave, you're going to have to throw

us out. But if I beat you, you're going to tell me everything about your research—what you've done in that secret room and what it is you're trying to do."

Russell was silent.

"I don't like mysteries," Edward said, "and this is one I'm going to get to the bottom of."

Russell's response was a derisive snort.

Like the night before, the two faced off on the stone tiles of the courtyard.

"Al, stand back."

"Standing back," reported Alphonse, glancing back at the wall they had climbed over to get onto the grounds. "I'll make sure our escape route's clear."

"You do that."

With those words, the battle began.

Neither combatant felt the need to test the other's strength this time, and both their goals were clear: Russell wanted Edward to leave town, and Edward wanted information from Russell. With the two so evenly matched and equally motivated, no one could say who would prevail. The only thing that was certain was that they would both be tested to their limit.

Russell lifted something in his hand, an iron vessel of some sort that he had grabbed from the laboratory. He brought his hands together, and it became a shiny black lump. Rapidly, the lump twisted into a sword many times larger than the original vessel.

"Ignoring conservation of mass? Rely on that Stone in your pocket like that, and you'll never beat me," snarled Edward. He brought his hands together, then pulled his left hand away, as if drawing a sword, and the auto-mail in his right arm extended until it became a long, sharp blade. "The bigger they are, the harder they break!" Edward shouted, waving his slender arm-blade at Russell's giant iron sword.

Edward lunged forward, slicing the air with his arm-blade. Russell caught the blade with his own, blocking the swing in midair.

Russell gasped and took a step back. He had been counting on his larger weapon giving him the advantage, but now he saw a fracture clearly running down the iron blade from the spot where Edward had caught it with his arm-blade.

"What's wrong?" Edward taunted him. "Go ahead, use your Stone again! See what good it does you!"

Russell put his hand on the back of his thick sword and twisted around, trying to knock Edward backwards, sword-arm and all—but it was merely a ruse. As he turned, he brought his leg up in a swift circle-kick, catching Edward squarely on the shoulder.

"Yow!" Edward shouted as he was knocked back by the blow. Before Edward had time to regain his balance, Russell ran to the outside of the laboratory and put his hands to the wall.

Edward braced himself for a volley of stone spikes like the ones they had launched at each other the night before, but

Russell lifted his hands to reveal a tiny, tiny . . .

. . . *door?*

Edward glared at him suspiciously as Russell grabbed the door's handle. The instant before it opened, Edward remembered what was on the other side of that wall. Twisting his body in midair, he fell back and to the side as a blast of flame erupted from the opening. Russell had opened a door directly into the laboratory furnace.

"Whoa! That was close!" Edward yelped as he fell on his rear to avoid the blast. As he struggled to stand, he saw Russell's foot flying straight at him. Edward dodged aside at the last moment, thinking quickly enough to thrust with his right arm-blade at the same time. Russell's eyes went to the shining steel, and Edward's left fist caught him in the side.

"Got you!"

"No, I've got you!" shouted Russell, grabbing Edward's outstretched fist. Russell leaned into Edward's shoulder and fell onto him, pushing him toward the ground.

"Hey!" Edward reached a hand down to the stone surface of the courtyard and lurched sideways, rolling out from under Russell. Edward hopped up and away, putting some distance between them. Russell let him go, choosing to catch his breath rather than give chase.

"You're as shifty as a little monkey," he sneered.

"What did you say!?"

"But for a monkey, you've got a pretty good punch," Russell admitted, rubbing his side. Edward grinned, then winced and rubbed his own shoulder, which had taken the brunt of Russell's kick a moment before.

The two had adopted a similar strategy. They knew that when it came to straight alchemy, they were evenly matched. The deadly weapons they had fashioned were only for feinting to create opportunities to land a few blows in hand-to-hand combat. But there too, they were evenly matched.

"We'll be at this until the sun comes up," Russell said, sounding as unconcerned as if he were talking about two strangers.

"You wish! You're only a match for me because of that Stone, remember?" Edward shouted, furious that Russell actually considered himself his equal.

"That kick wasn't alchemy, you know," Russell said with a smile.

"I know," Edward spat. Okay, so maybe they were equally matched when it came to fighting, but he didn't have to remind him with every other breath. "Would you stop being so . . . so annoying?"

"I'm not annoying. You're just easily annoyed."

Edward feinted and kicked. Russell deftly stepped aside, bringing his elbow down toward Edward's back.

"Saw that one coming!" Edward yelled, twisting away as he brought his knee up to score a blow into Russell's solar plexus.

Russell froze for an instant, the wind knocked out of him. Edward pushed him down, trying to pin him without actually hurting him too much, but Russell easily knocked his hand aside. Edward shook his hand out to get rid of the tingling from the blow he had inflicted.

"Not bad."

"Same to you," Russell countered as he tried to catch his breath and rubbed his sore stomach. "For someone with a short temper, you sure are persistent."

"Hurts, doesn't it? I spar with my brother every day, you know. That's the difference training makes. When I get a blow in, you can bet you'll feel it."

"Yeah, well . . . I only fight grown men, myself. I suppose I should do some sparring with Fletcher, now that you mention it."

"Huh? Fletcher can fight?" Edward couldn't picture lanky, frail Fletcher being much of a challenge. Russell laughed.

"It would be good practice for fighting someone *shorter* than myself."

Edward's temples twitched. "You really, really shouldn't have said that."

"Ah-hah! So that bothers you!" chortled Russell. He seemed very satisfied with himself for having hit his mark. "You shouldn't let it, you know," he added. His tone made it clear he meant the exact opposite.

Edward howled with rage and came at him, fists swinging. Russell wasn't the type to be caught by wild punches. He ducked aside and brought up his leg, but Edward was more focused than he seemed, and he dodged the kick easily.

"I'm going to beat you to a pulp!" he shouted. "Then I'll do this, and this, and sn-n-n-nap!" Edward leapt around and waved his hands as he spoke, pantomiming how he was going to pick Russell up and break him over his knee. The snapping noise was the part where he broke the imaginary Russell in half. "I never liked you, not from the moment I saw you. You act like you're so smooth, but you just come across as uptight and stuck-up. Yeah, I'm sure it gets you places, but you know what? It makes you seem like a grown-up. Of course, you could be lying about your age . . . "

Russell's mouth twitched when he heard the word "grown-up." Edward noticed and went in for the kill. Finally the tables had turned, and he had a lot to get even for.

"Oh? So you're touchy about your age? Maybe I should put it another way? You're not like a 'grown-up,' you're . . . past your prime!" Edward laughed. "I'm sorry, did I hurt your feelings? How old are you really?"

Edward was on a roll. Now *he* was the smooth talker, while Russell looked positively miserable. Until . . .

"Aha!" Russell exclaimed with a wide grin. "You can't stand my being taller than you, even though we're the same age!" He took a step forward. "You *want* me to be older than you, don't you?"

Edward cringed, but he wasn't going to give up so easily. "You're behind the times, out of style, past your prime . . .

And you don't have enough energy to be the same age as me!" He took a step forward and pointed an accusatory finger at Russell. The two started in on each other at point-blank range.

"I'm going to wipe that smirk off your face!"

"Keep chattering, little monkey."

Sparks shot through the air between them.

They faced off, one looking down, the other looking up, as the insults continued to fly.

"You'll pay for using my name, I swear. And don't worry, I won't take pity on you just 'cause you're an *old geezer!*"

Russell raised clenched fists, rubbed his eyes, and yawned. "Phew! Sure is tiring looking down at someone for so long. I guess you wouldn't understand . . ."

In just a few moments, the two had completely forgotten their objectives. This was personal.

The fight escalated with alchemy, punches, and flying kicks. The only difference was that now they hurled insults at each other as they battled.

They both knew they were being ridiculous. But when they looked around, they saw that neither of their brothers were there to stop them . . . so on they fought.

WHILE THE OLDER BROTHERS battled it out, Alphonse worked his way down the wall to make sure their escape route was clear. "Uh-oh," he muttered to himself, dropping down to all fours as several guards passed by. When they had arrived there had only been three guards at the front gate. But now those three had been joined by a few more. He could hear them pacing outside the perimeter. If they scaled the wall, they would be caught in an instant.

Alphonse looked across the compound to the wall on the other side. If memory served, it was strung along its length with barbed wire. This could work to their advantage. If the guards relied on the barbed wire, they might not patrol that side. No guard would want to give chase over barbed wire, but for Edward with his steel arm, and Alphonse in his armor, a barrier like that posed little difficulty. Besides, it was beginning to look like their only option.

Alphonse sat up on his haunches. One of the trees lining the far wall had begun to shake.

Guards? In the courtyard?

Alphonse was straining to make out what was going on, when the piercing shriek of a guard whistle cut the night air. Back at the mansion, lights flickered on, one by one. Alphonse froze. Then someone hissed his name.

"Alphonse!"

It was Fletcher, standing before the wall with the barbed wire. That's what had made the tree shake: Fletcher climbing down it.

"Fletcher?"

"Quick, get your brother! If you don't leave right now, you'll get caught!"

"Right!"

Alphonse could tell from the look on Fletcher's face that he was serious. This wasn't a trap—he really wanted to help them escape.

Meanwhile, Edward and Russell were wasting their alchemy talents throwing chunks of courtyard at each other. Suddenly, another guard's whistle sounded.

"What the—? Al!" Edward tossed away the cobblestone in his hand, and turned to see lights flashing on in the mansion. Russell saw the guards approaching swiftly.

"I told them to stay out of this!"

"Well, looks like they weren't listening!" Edward broke into a run. He could hear Alphonse calling from the back of the courtyard.

"Ed! This way!'

"Al!"

"W-wait!" shouted Russell, giving chase.

"What are you following me for?" Edward yelled over his shoulder.

"I'm going to be the one who kicks you out! I've got my reputation to consider!"

"You're just scared we'll get caught and blow your cover!"

The two followed Alphonse to the back of the courtyard until they reached the rear wall, where Fletcher was waiting.

"Fletcher!" exclaimed Russell. "What are you doing here? I told you to handle Mugear!"

Ignoring his brother, Fletcher turned and put his hands

to the wall behind him. An alchemical transmutation circle had been drawn on the wall. When he touched it, a light flared from inside the circle and rapidly spread across the wall. When it faded, a door stood where there had been nothing but solid stone.

"Quick, go through! There aren't any guards on the other side—I checked."

Edward and Alphonse looked at Fletcher with amazement.

"Fletcher—you can do alchemy?"

"And without a Stone! You're better than Russell."

Fletcher pushed them both toward the door.

"Hurry up and get out of here! If you get caught, we'll all be in trouble. Please!"

Fletcher's urgency was easy to understand. If Edward and Alphonse were caught, they would give their names, and the impostors would be unveiled. Of course, it wasn't like they owed Fletcher and Russell anything. After all, *they* were the ones who had stolen the real Elric brothers' identities. Still, the desperation in Fletcher's voice touched them, and without thinking, they instinctively threw open the door and ran through it.

Behind them, on the other side of the wall, they heard the muffled sound of a commotion. But where they stood it was frightfully quiet. There were no guards anywhere to be seen.

"Thrown out on our ear again."

"Yup."

"I don't like how any of this is going," Edward muttered, rubbing the bruise on his cheek where Russell had landed a punch. "No Stone, no research data . . . We're taking the fall for Russell's scheme, and the townspeople are all backward . . . Come to think of it, why are we staying here, anyway? I don't care if this town is ruined!"

Standing quietly next to him, Alphonse nodded. "You're right. Russell doesn't have the Stone. But . . . he did have some trial Stones that work. There aren't any useful research notes. But . . . they do have the Water of Life. And Fletcher does seem to regret stealing our identities. And even the townspeople are beginning to realize they can't keep doing whatever Mugear tells them to forever. Sure, it won't affect us one way or the other if this town dries up and blows away, but it would still be a shame, wouldn't it? I mean, it feels like we're standing at a crossroads. So much could happen, for good or bad . . . "

Edward glanced at Alphonse out of the corner of his eye.

Alphonse returned his sidelong glance. "Come on, don't you care about this town a little?"

"Well, if you put it that way . . . "

"I'm just saying what I see in your eyes, Ed."

The two looked back up at the wall. It was completely quiet again. They had no idea what was happening on the other side. For that matter, they had no idea what had been going on in there before, or what the impostor Elrics were really up to.

"Not interested in the Stone or gold . . ." Edward mulled over Russell's words. "So what does he want?"

"He really gets to you, doesn't he?"

Well, thought Edward, *if nothing else, at least we'll have plenty of time to guess tonight.*

WITH A WAVE of Fletcher's hand, the door disappeared, leaving the wall in its original state. He turned to his brother, his eyes fixed on his feet. "I'm sorry."

Russell's face was set in his usual mask, but he was furious. Yet when he spoke, his voice remained cool and even. "You mean you're sorry you let them go? No need to apologize. It's a good thing they didn't get caught and tell Mugear who they were. Then we'd be in real trouble, huh?"

"I'm not talking about that."

And you know it, but you're too mad to even say it.

Fletcher swallowed. "I'm sorry I used alchemy."

His brother's eyes burned into his, and Fletcher had to turn his face aside. He had promised . . .

Russell sighed deeply and turned away. "What would Father think? He asked us never to use alchemy. We promised! I . . . I hoped that you, at least, would keep that promise."

Fletcher stared at his brother's back. Come to think of it,

in a number of ways, he felt he hadn't looked straight into his brother's eyes since their arrival at the lab. He couldn't bear to.

I don't want to see you lie.

I don't want to see you using the Stone . . . using alchemy.

I don't want to see you drown in your research . . .

But now it seemed to Fletcher that he could see chains around his brother, chains binding his thoughts and his actions. They were wrapped so tightly Russell could barely breathe—yet he couldn't see them. All this time Fletcher had thought he was the one who was trapped, forced to go along with his brother's lies, but now he could see it was the other way around. Russell was bound; Fletcher was free, and only Fletcher could see the truth. But how could Russell be freed?

He was lying to make someone *else*'s dreams come true.

He was devoting his life to research to finish what someone *else* could not.

He was using alchemy, all the while apologizing for it to that someone *else*.

"Can't you see?" Fletcher whispered.

"See what?"

"Why did we lie and say we were the Elric brothers?"

"We had to so we could do our research here."

"And why are we doing this research?"

"Because it's what he wanted. He wanted to redeem this town."

"If you think that's what he wanted you to do, why don't you just use your own alchemy instead of those Stones?"

"Because he told me not to."

Russell can't see the chains . . .

"Does it make you happy, doing all this for him?"

"I'm doing the right thing."

The chains are so heavy.

"If that's true," Fletcher shouted, his voice trembling, "why do you look so miserable!?"

Fletcher was filled with pity for his brother. It was time to give a name to those chains. "You're not our father!"

Russell's face hardened.

"Our father was a great man," Fletcher continued, "and a talented alchemist. We started doing alchemy because we wanted to be like him, remember? But when he told us to stop, we did." Fletcher's voice choked. His entire body was trembling, and he was on the verge of tears. "You told me it was all right to lie to get into this lab so we could carry on what our father started. But you're pushing yourself too far with those Stones—and for what? For who? You're just following the same path that he walked! Why, Russell? What about what *you* want?"

Russell said nothing.

"Our father had the talent—he even made apprentice to a State Alchemist. But then he quit and came to do research here. He had his reasons, I'm sure, but all the same, he didn't want you to follow in his footsteps. Russ, if you keep on like this, you'll kill yourself . . ."

The two brothers had dreamed of becoming alchemists, just like the one they most looked up to, their father. But he had ordered them to give up their dream. It would have been hard on anyone.

"You think Father would be angry at me for using alchemy like I did just now? How do you think he'd feel about us stealing the Elrics' names? I used alchemy to help them, and if I can use my talent to help others, then I'll keep on using it. In fact, someday, I want to be an alchemist—a great alchemist."

Russell stared at Fletcher. Fletcher cringed. Would he shout at him? Would he punch him? He'd done both. But Fletcher wouldn't turn away. His brother was wrapped in chains he couldn't see, and it was Fletcher's responsibility to set him free. He returned Russell's gaze, and his heart filled with courage. This was what Alphonse had given him at the pharmacy. It was a fair trade.

IN THE END, Russell said and did nothing. He just turned away. And then a guard appeared and told them to report to the main hall. Without a word, Russell began walking back toward the mansion.

"Russ . . . ?" Fletcher followed, watching his brother out of the corner of his eye.

Russell's face was white in the moonlight, an emotionless mask. Suddenly their positions had reversed. Now it was Russell who couldn't talk, Russell who had been silenced by Fletcher's words.

As they entered the hall, they saw Mugear halfway up the staircase to the second floor, leaning on the banister. He was looking over some documents. He glanced over at Russell and Fletcher when they entered.

"So you drove off the bandits?"

Russell nodded. "Yes."

"That's two nights in a row. This is beginning to disturb my rest. You tell me we should merely drive them off, Master Edward, but perhaps it would be better to capture them?"

"No. They can perform a little alchemy. If we brought them inside, who knows what havoc they might wreak? If we keep driving them off, they'll give up eventually." Russell spoke quickly and without hesitation.

Mugear shook his head. "No, I think not. I believe you're worried that I'll meet them and your deception will be revealed."

Russell tensed. Beside him, Fletcher gasped.

"You instructed me to take shelter in the cellar, so I did, but I had so much time on my hands down there . . . Plenty of time to think things over."

Mugear came down the stairs, sliding his hand down the railing. "The cellar of this house was made for holding people who wouldn't listen to reason, you see. I was just thinking about the last person I put in there."

Russell swallowed and said nothing.

"He was a man from this town, in fact. He left years before to study alchemy at the capital. He had great talent, but for some reason, he returned despite having just begun his apprenticeship. I'm not sure of the details of his departure, but he seemed very frightened. I offered him safe haven, and in exchange, he agreed to make me a Philosopher's Stone. He said he was through with alchemy, but when he saw how shabby his hometown had become, he agreed to do research for me, as long as I permitted him to continue his work on the Water of Life. He said the Water would help restore the greenery that this town had lost so long ago.

"My intentions were noble. If he had completed the Philosopher's Stone, I would have used my influence to make certain the military didn't come after him, and I allowed him to do as much of his own research as he liked. I was generous, too. I gave him all the materials he requested. However, all he did was repeat the same experiments over and over, to no purpose. He would not listen to reason, so I put him down in the cellar for a while to think things over."

Mugear held Russell and Fletcher in his steady gaze as he spoke. "I remember he told me he had two sons. Brothers with golden hair and silver eyes. He would smile as he told me how they resembled their late mother. When he completed the Philosopher's Stone, he said, he would say *adieu* to his life of toil and summon his sons to him to share in the paradise of Xenotime. His name was . . . ah, yes, Nash Tringum, I believe."

Mugear threw down the documents he was holding. They drifted to rest at Russell's feet. The documents identified State Alchemist Edward Elric.

"Apparently the real Edward has gold hair and golden eyes." Mugear strode over, grabbed Russell's chin, and tilted it up. "Your eyes don't look gold to me." He swung his fist back and hit Russell hard on the jaw. Russell fell to the floor.

"You're Nash's sons, aren't you!?" Mugear snarled.

Russell just sat on the floor without lifting a hand to defend himself and said nothing.

"The ones who came here—these bandits of yours—I know they're the real Elric brothers. I'll bring them here and have them prove it." He grabbed Russell by the lapels. But Russell's face remained a mask, as always. Mugear raised his fist again and hissed, "Insolent child!"

The fist fell on Fletcher, who leapt between Mugear and his brother.

"Please, stop!" begged Fletcher. His head began to pound. "It's just as you say. I'm Fletcher! And this is my brother, Russell. Nash Tringum was our father!"

"Fletcher!" Russell pulled his brother to him, and saw the bruise forming on his forehead. He shot Mugear a furious look, but by then, they were surrounded by guards.

"Throw them in the cellar!" Mugear ordered. The guards pinned Russell's arms behind him and shoved him toward the stairs leading downward.

"Oh," Mugear said with a smile. "I almost forgot." Reaching into Russell's pocket, he pulled out a faintly glowing red shard. "I see you've gotten some use out of your trial Stones. You might even be able to make a little gold, no?"

Mugear grabbed a candle and studied the reflections in the Stone. For a moment, he was lost in fascination as he gazed upon the shimmering light. "I'll have to summon new alchemists to complete my project, and I'll have to raise more money to fund their research. Things will be hectic around here."

He cared nothing for the townspeople, whose lives would only grow harder as he continued to bleed them to fund his project. Mugear's only interest was the obscene wealth he dreamed of acquiring for himself with a true Philosopher's Stone.

Chapter Three

Crimson Water

EDWARD spent the next morning fretting over what he would do if Mugear had them followed.

And then one of the mansion guards appeared at their encampment.

"Good morning. I'm glad I found you."

The guard's greeting took Edward by surprise. He appeared to be sincere. After what had transpired the night before, Alphonse and Edward had decided it would be too much of an imposition to stay at Belsio's place again, so they had camped a little distance outside town. This poor man must have been running around frantically since dawn trying to find them.

"Let me guess—you're here to arrest us, right?" Edward said.

"Absolutely not! My employer, Master Mugear, would like to apologize to Master Edward for any inconvenience caused by the impostors. In fact, he'd like to invite you to the mansion so that he may have the opportunity to apologize to you in person."

Edward gaped. *"Master" Edward? Me?*

"S-so you found out about us—or rather, you found out about the other two?"

"Yes, sir. Don't worry, we're keeping the impostors under lock and key in the mansion cellar." The guard smiled. "They won't bother you again, Master Edward, Master Alphonse." He nodded to the brothers in turn.

Edward and Alphonse looked at each other. Neither of them had much enjoyed being ridiculed by the townspeople, but now that the tables had turned, they couldn't bring themselves to gloat.

The guard led them back to the mansion grounds, which they entered through the front gate for the first time. When they arrived, Mugear greeted them personally. They had launched two assaults on his residence and heard much about its owner from the townspeople, but this was their first meeting with the man himself. Yet he smiled at them as though he'd know them for years.

"Welcome to my humble abode, Master Edward and Master Alphonse. I must apologize for the inconvenience this whole affair has caused you. I feel somewhat responsible . . . Might I make it up to you with a meal?"

Mugear led them personally into his lavishly decorated dining hall. Edward tapped Alphonse on the shoulder and whispered, "He wants us to do research for him!"

"I bet you're right," Alphonse whispered back.

Mugear turned and gave them a winning smile. The fact that he hadn't mentioned their two incursions onto his property made it clear that he had an ulterior motive. They sat down at his table, where a hot meal was brought before them. Edward began to eat while enduring the full force of Mugear's beaming smile.

"Those impostors certainly had me fooled!" Mugear exclaimed. "I regret that you unjustly suffered the censure they deserve." He raised an eyebrow at Edward. "Won't your brother have something to eat?"

Alphonse politely excused himself from partaking in the meal as Mugear launched into his explanation about the impostors. He told them the boys were the sons of a man he had previously employed. He avoided implicating himself in the matter. Edward took a sip of vegetable soup and interrupted him.

"Er, you do know that we broke into your property, right? Twice. Are you sure you don't want to throw *us* in the cellar too?"

"Wouldn't dream of it!" Mugear said, still smiling broadly. "The only reason you did so was because you learned of the impostors and wished to set matters straight, no? Why, I certainly can't blame you for that!"

So he was going to overlook their transgressions—perhaps

in return for them overlooking his own highly illegal plans to transmute gold.

"I have to wonder, though . . . What I am to do now that I have no alchemists? Where will I find someone to replace them? Someone skilled enough to fashion a Philosopher's Stone?"

"Do you mean us?" Edward asked bluntly, cutting to the chase.

Mugear scratched his cheek and appeared embarrassed. "I would offer you forty percent of all the profits. In return for you not notifying the State, of course . . ."

"Oh, keeping it a secret wouldn't be a problem," Edward assured him with a conspiratorial smile.

"It would only be until we excavate a new gold vein in town. This community has all the mining equipment it needs to dig real gold. It's just that . . . it's been quite arduous trying to find that next vein."

"And expensive, I'd wager," Edward added with mock concern. Mugear didn't seem to notice.

"Well, what do you think? I'd guess that—as a scientist— you would leap at the opportunity to work on creating a Philosopher's Stone, yes?"

"Well . . . "

Of course Edward had no intention of working for Mugear, but he wanted to glean some more information before letting on. And besides, he enjoyed watching Mugear squirm.

"Is there a problem?"

"No, no, just . . . it's a point of pride with me not to step into someone else's work midstream. Maybe you could tell me a little more about this Nash alchemist?"

"Ah, now, there was a talent! He even received a posting at a military facility as the apprentice to a renowned State Alchemist."

"If he was so talented, why did he disappear? I'm sure you offered him protection from the military too, in case he succeeded in making a Stone . . ."

"Yes, well . . ." Mugear appeared to be choosing his words carefully to avoid saying anything that might implicate him. "To make a Stone requires a great deal of trial and error, no? You need to experiment with all manner of methods and materials. However, Nash failed to distinguish himself as a researcher of great caliber. He ignored my suggestions, and, not wishing to waste my limited research funds, I had him think things over for a while in the cellar. Of course, being an alchemist, he fashioned a door and escaped quite readily."

Edward snorted.

"After that, the few alchemists remaining on staff attempted a variety of experiments, but they quickly lost the thread of his research. That's when Russell and his brother arrived. Russell claimed that the distillation process they had been using was wrong—or something like that—and he succeeded in making some progress with the test samples his father had abandoned."

Edward and Alphonse nodded, impressed. If it was true, Russell had accomplished quite a feat. To fashion even a trial Stone from his father's work without a list of materials or methodology was no mean feat.

"However," continued Mugear, "failure after failure reduced our remaining materials to a handful. So he attempted to learn how Nash made his creations."

"I see."

Mugear looked at Edward eagerly. "Well, what do you say? Will you join me? Can you decipher what went into making the Water?"

Edward frowned and rubbed his chin. From what he had seen last night, he was certain that reverse-engineering the Water would be impossible. He kept that information to himself.

"We'd have to talk to Russell, wouldn't we, Al?"

Alphonse nodded. "It's the only way," he agreed.

"May we?" Edward guessed correctly that Mugear wouldn't refuse them such a simple request, especially when he believed he was so close to acquiring new talent to work on his research.

"Of course, of course," Mugear answered with a smile. "They're behaving themselves in the cellar right now. Russell can perform a bit of alchemy, of course, so I posted a guard."

Mugear offered to take them down, that broad smile still pasted on his face.

THE AIR in the cellar was cool.

Mugear opened a heavy iron door to reveal a corridor running down the center of the room, with cells on either side.

"The far one on the right."

The guard posted in front of the door was notice enough. Edward and Alphonse asked to speak to the impostors alone. They stepped inside, and the iron door closed heavily behind them.

In the cell, they found Russell and Fletcher seated behind a wall of bars, their wrists bound in handcuffs.

"Edward! Alphonse!" Fletcher saw them first and came running up to the bars.

"Fletcher! You're hurt!" Edward burst out, seeing the bruise on the younger boy's temple.

"It's nothing. I . . . " Fletcher lowered his eyes. "I know it's late to be saying this, but . . . We're really sorry. Really."

Behind him, Russell sat in silence, not even looking up at their visitors.

"Hey, Russell, you seem kind of down. Where's all that youthful energy from last night?" Edward teased. Russell didn't move.

"Why have you come?" he asked in a low voice.

"Mugear asked us to. From the sound of it, he wants us to pick up where you left off. Man, he's even slimier than I thought!"

"So? Are you going to do it?"

"Well, he offered to give us forty percent of the profits, and I *do* want to make a Philosopher's Stone . . . "

"It's going to cost a lot more money than that . . . And you've seen how hard life is for the townspeople already."

"That didn't stop *you.*"

Russell frowned. "I . . . " Russell began to rise, but then just as suddenly sank back down. "I was doing it for them."

"So you were making a Stone, limitless gold . . . all for the townspeople?"

"Yes, the Stone and . . . the Water of Life." Russell's voice grew fainter and fainter. Everything he had done, everything he had worked for—it was all over. He shut his mouth tightly, unwilling to give voice to his failure.

"So wait," Edward continued, thinking out loud. "This Water of Life—you made it to bring greenery back to the village? I suppose that would help the people." Edward put his hands on the bars. "You really thought you were doing the right thing?"

Russell didn't respond.

"Say it, Russell."

Russell was silent. Edward took his hands off the bars and leaned back against the opposite wall. "Your father was Nash

Tringum, right? He worked in some military lab? You need to be good to make it to a place like that. Your father must have been pretty talented. That explains you knowing all the alchemy you do . . . and Fletcher being able to use it too.

"So," continued Edward, "you wanted to be like your father."

Russell gave a drawn-out sigh. "I wanted to . . . But look what happened." He raised his shackled hands. "What about *your* father, Edward?"

Edward's face twisted into a scowl. He had little good to say about his father. "Who knows? I can't even say if he's dead or alive."

"So he's missing—like ours." Russell leaned back against the wall. He looked tired. "We were born in a town far away from here. Our father spent his days studying alchemy, and I wanted to become an alchemist like him. He wasn't a strong man, but he knew more about alchemy than anyone. He wasn't that good at performing it, but in the lab, his skills were second to none. He always said he wanted to use his knowledge to help people—or, at least, to support another alchemist who could practice the art to help others.

"That's why he apprenticed himself to a famous alchemist in a military lab. But something about the application of their methods disagreed with him. He couldn't take it anymore, so one day, he took off. After that, our whole family lived every day as fugitives. Our father lived in a state of constant fear. He used to tell us over and over that he was through with alchemy. He made us promise to never touch the stuff."

"Where was this military facility?" Edward asked.

"I don't know. He would never tell me."

"Too bad," Edward said. "I guess I won't be able to pick up his trail there, then. What about your mother?"

"Our mother died. She was so exhausted from all that running . . . After she was gone, our father told us there was a town he wanted to show us—the town where he was born. He told us to wait on the outskirts while he went ahead to scout things out. If it looked like there was a place for us there, he would send word."

Fletcher looked sad. Listening to his brother talk about his father, their life as fugitives, and the breakup of their family was painful. He had his share of hard memories.

"Our father sent us a postcard," Russell continued. "He said he'd found work here. There was a good lab, one where he could study in peace, where the military wouldn't find him.

"He said he'd come get us . . . " Russell paused. "I'm sure he had a reason for leaving, but he never told me what it was. We never saw him again."

After a pause, Russell went on. "This was his home. I wanted to make it like it was when he was young—green, and full of life. I don't know where he went, but I thought that would give him a reason to come back. The Water of Life was the key. With it, we could bring the green back, and the townspeople would see that there was more to life than just goldsmithing."

"So that's what you were trying to do." Everything was finally starting to make sense to Edward and Alphonse. But for all of Mugear's ambitions, Russell's hopes, and the townspeople's dreams, nothing had come of any of it.

"I thought I was following in my father's footsteps, but in the end, I was going nowhere. I just wanted to do something for this town, to make my father proud," Russell said bitterly.

Edward didn't try to comfort him. "Maybe you were going about it the wrong way."

"Huh?"

"If you want to help the townspeople, you don't need a Philosopher's Stone or the Water of Life. You have two hands—use them. If you want to make the town green, start moving rocks. I'm sure that would make your father proud." Edward grasped the bars of their cell. "Whatever happens, you're not going to get anything done by sitting here moping. You've got to move on. Don't make me ashamed of you, okay? Especially if you're going to use my name!"

The bars suddenly bent in Edward's hands. Edward stepped through the gap into their cell, went to the prisoners, and broke their handcuffs. He walked out without so much as looking back. He wouldn't pull them out by the hand. When they went, it would be of their own free will.

"Let's go, Al."

Alphonse nodded. He glanced back at the bars, bent wide enough for a boy to easily walk through. Inside the cell, Fletcher stood close to his brother. He noticed Alphonse looking at him, and lifted his chin. His eyes filled with strength.

Alphonse gave him a nod. He knew that even if Russell resisted, Fletcher would get himself and his brother out of there. He would take them to a better place and find a new way. Satisfied, Alphonse turned and left.

"RUSSELL," Fletcher said softly. "The cell's open. Our handcuffs are off. If we're going to leave, we have to decide now."

Russell stared silently at his hands resting on his knees.

"I'm getting out of this place," Fletcher continued, "and I'm going to apologize to the townspeople. Then I'm going to learn more alchemy. I'm going to get really good at it. We might not be able to turn this place into a paradise overnight, but we can sure help move some rocks. You know, Russ, maybe you'll like that kind of work more than alchemy."

Russell looked surprised.

"Do you know what this means?" Fletcher asked. "You're not in chains anymore. You don't have to follow in Father's footsteps anymore. You can do what you want. You don't have to hold yourself back!"

"Fletcher . . . Since when did you become the older brother?"

"You know," Fletcher replied, "you always looked up to Father, but there's someone I look up to, too. I think to myself, 'If it will help him, I can be stronger.'"

Russell raised an eyebrow.

"Maybe you don't know this," Fletcher continued, "but I've always looked up to you."

Russell glanced into his brother's eyes and smiled. He stood up and put his hand on Fletcher's head. "You've grown."

It was a familiar gesture. He used to do it all the time when their family was still together. He would put his hand on Fletcher's head and say "You've grown," and his eyes would say *but you better not get taller than me*. Fletcher would look up at him and reply, "Watch out! I'm gaining on you!" and the two would laugh.

Today, Fletcher knew that Russell was talking about more than just height. Feeling his brother's hand on his head, Fletcher smiled. "Watch out, I'm gaining on you."

The two walked out through the bent bars. They would go apologize to the townspeople. They would accept their punishment, and then they would help restore the land to its former verdure.

AS THEY WALKED through the bars, the mansion's main hall rang with laughter. One of Mugear's servants was passing him chunks of broken rock, which he proceeded to turn into gold. "Ha, ha! Even I, who know so little of alchemy, can do wonders with this Stone!" Though he knew the gold would only last for a moment, watching the rock transform before his eyes had become an addiction. He couldn't stop transmuting.

"We may not have much Water left, but it's more than enough to continue my research. With that genius Edward working for me, I'll have a Philosopher's Stone completed in no time . . . And when the townspeople see the gold I make, no one will think I'm squandering their money." Mugear rocked back and forth with glee. He was very pleased with himself. He was about to perform more transmutations when he heard a voice call out behind him.

"And when the gold is gone, the townspeople will be as badly off as they were when they started."

"Master Edward!" Mugear turned to see Edward standing behind him.

"So this all the Water you have left, huh?"

Mugear gasped. Edward held the flask in his hand. It sloshed audibly as he rocked it from side to side. "I find it hard to respect a man who would hold a whole town hostage for just a few drops of liquid." Edward looked around. "This mansion of yours—it's pretty lavish. Where'd you get the money to pay for all this? I suppose you've been skimming off the top of the proceeds of the mine and the research funding all along . . . Yeah, that would make sense."

Mugear didn't even hear Edward's rebuke. His eyes were fixed on the gently sloshing Water in the flask in Edward's hand. "Master Edward, please . . . give the Water back to me! Without it, my research is finished!"

Edward stepped aside deftly, avoiding Mugear's grasping hands. "Your research is finished anyway. You have no data, no methodology . . . The fact that you even got this far using someone else's half-finished experiments is a miracle."

"Please, don't say that," Mugear begged. "Ah! It's the money, isn't it? How does *fifty* percent of the proceeds sound, eh?" Mugear seemed to think Edward's refusal to work for him was just a negotiation tactic.

"Actually," Edward said, "there is something that's been bothering me."

"What's that?" Mugear asked, the smile returning to his face.

"You."

Mugear coughed. "What?"

"I don't believe you would just let Nash walk out of here in the middle of his research—and with all of his research notes, at that."

"Oh, those? Nash disposed of them. There was nothing to take."

"Uh-huh," Edward nodded. "So where's Nash now? If he didn't have any notes, you would have gotten everything you could out of him before you let him go. But you didn't . . . So what gives? He didn't leave, did he?"

A scowl darkened Mugear's face.

"Where is he? In another one of your cells?"

"He's not here," Mugear said, flinching under Edward's hard gaze.

"Not here? So you just let him go? Or else . . . No, you didn't!" Edward finally figured it out. "You killed him!"

Mugear's silence was as good as any confession.

"Is there no limit to your greed?"

"I simply asked him where his research materials were," Mugear blurted out. "And I might have tried to soften him up a little. He didn't have a strong constitution, you see . . . "

"What?" Edward cut him off. "You think that absolves you?" Edward was furious. "Sure, the townspeople and Russell deserve some of the blame for what's been going on around here, but I knew from the start that you were the worst of the bunch. And to think I was going to cut you some slack." Edward ground his teeth. "Not anymore."

Mugear seemed unruffled. "You would judge me?"

"No, the courts will do that. I just want to kick your ass."

"I'm afraid neither of those options appeals to me much. There will be no trial. I will take back my Water. And, I rather think that, with *this*, I can defeat a State Alchemist."

Mugear held up the glimmering red Stone. "Sorry, but there's no chance of you leaving."

Mugear thrust his hands onto the railing of the stairs. There was the telltale flash of an alchemical transmutation, and when he lifted his arms, he was cradling a giant rifle. By the time he swung around the huge, two-barreled cannon, Edward had already shaped his right arm into a sword.

"Come and get me, alchemist! I'll turn you into a honeycomb before you get within arm's reach of me!" Mugear shouted. Laughing maniacally, he began firing his gun.

Edward ducked behind a thick pillar. Mugear fired at it, chipping the plaster. "You can't hide from me!"

"Keep shooting and you might just hit something!" Edward yelled, covering his ears against the roaring of the gun. He waited until the stream of bullets had eaten away half the pillar, then swung his arm-sword fast. It sliced clean through the rest of the pillar.

"What the—!?"

Edward cupped one hand to his mouth and shouted, "Tim-m-m-ber!" He didn't intend for the pillar to crush Mugear, but it would force him to scramble out of the way. Mugear would be easy enough to catch in the ensuing rubble. Mugear stared wide-eyed as the pillar began its descent. As it fell, it took a section of the ceiling with it, raining chunks of stone upon the floor.

Edward stepped back to the safety of the entryway and watched the pillar fall. "There she goes . . . Now where is he?" Edward swung his arms around, trying to clear some of the roiling plaster dust that filled the air. He expected Mugear to have ducked into the corner by the stairwell to avoid the pillar, but he wasn't there. Edward was just craning his neck to check behind a pile of rubble when he heard a crunching sound to his right.

"Huh?"

Just below the spot where the pillar had landed, a low dome hugged the floor. As Edward watched, the dome split in two, shoving fragments of the pillar to either side. From beneath the dome Mugear emerged, a new gun in his hand.

"Crafty of you to drop that pillar on me," he said as he pulled the trigger.

"Whoa!" Edward leapt and rolled to the side as the muzzle of Mugear's new weapon tracked him. The Stone gave Mugear the power to generate an endless stream of bullets.

Edward ducked behind a pile of rubble from the collapsed pillar, but the hail of gunfire soon tore away what little cover it provided. He turned and placed his hand on a nearby wall to create a spike, but that too was reduced to dust in moments. Edward was at a loss. The bullets were endless—it was like fighting a small army all at once.

"What's the matter? I'd have thought a State Alchemist would be more of a challenge!" Mugear laughed. He was fashioning an even larger cannon as he spoke.

"I'll show you what a State Alchemist can do!" Edward shouted, dashing toward Mugear. He moved so fast that he reached him before he could raise his cannon. With his arm-sword, Edward sliced the gun's barrel in two. Taken off guard, Mugear stumbled back. Edward saw his opportunity, clenched his other hand into a fist, and smacked Mugear in the jaw.

Mugear swore and began forming another cannon as Edward dodged back and planted his hand on the floor to form another wall. The stone of the floor arched up, revealing earth and the twisted roots of plants beneath. When the floor was perfectly vertical, Edward kicked it with all his strength. Seeing the wall toppling towards him, Mugear formed another half-dome to block its fall.

"Hah! You're wide open!" Edward shouted, running to grab the remaining stair railing. There was a flash of alchemical energy, and Edward pulled away a long, heavy pole. "I'll crack that dome in half!" he vowed, charging Mugear's shield. But as he brought his pole down as hard as he could, the top half disappeared with a horrible screech.

"Huh?" Edward gaped at the dome. Plaster dust hung white in the air. The dome opened before him, and there stood Mugear, bearing another cannon. He had completed it while sheltering inside the dome. Edward realized his pole hadn't disappeared—it had been vaporized by a blast of Mugear's firepower!

Mugear sat up inside the remaining ring of his dome-wall.

"Time to end this!" he shouted, as he squeezed the trigger.

The gun missed its mark. A great *Waboom!* echoed through the mansion as a giant cannonball smacked into the far side of the hall. Cracks ran through the wall and the entire room shuddered.

"Yikes!" Edward shouted. "This place is gonna come down!"

"Bah! I can build another mansion, but never again will I have the opportunity to put a State Alchemist in his place!" Mugear fired again and again. A cannonball landed at Edward's feet, knocking him off balance. Edward lurched to the side just as another flew straight at his face. At the last moment, he swung his arm-sword and cut the cannonball in half. A tingle ran up his arm and his shoulder went numb from the impact. He knew from the speed and weight that he had gotten lucky. He would not be able to knock the next shot aside. Running was not an option either. He would tire long before Mugear ran out of ammunition.

Edward threw up another wall, sturdier than the last, yet still it shook and cracked with every strike. Edward swore. "If only I could get closer, I'd have the upper hand."

Suddenly a door opened behind him and a voice called out, "Edward!" It was Russell. He took the devastation in with one glance and ran to his aid.

"Stay back, dummy!" Edward shouted over his shoulder. Bullets were flying everywhere. Before his wall completely disintegrated, Edward made a new one behind it while yelling to Russell, "Hide! Now! You'll just get in the way."

Mugear saw Russell and aimed a spray of bullets in his direction. "Too bad you don't have a Stone anymore! You won't be able to join in our little game." A giant cannonball hurtled through the air toward Russell. He dodged it by a hair and ran to Edward.

Another shot flew at them.

"Russell!" Edward shouted, taking his eyes off Mugear for a second. It was the moment Mugear had been waiting for.

"Now it ends!" he shouted triumphantly.

Just behind Edward, a spike rose from the floor and flew at him. Edward didn't have time to block its formation. He saw its deadly sharp point heading right for his eyes. Desperately, he swung his arm-sword and managed to cut off the tip, but it wasn't enough to stop the advance of the rest of the spike. Edward braced himself for an impact that was sure to kill him—but the malicious spike came to a halt not an inch before reaching him.

"Who was it you were saying would just get in the way?" asked a voice beside Edward.

"Russell?"

Russell stood with his arm stretched over Edward's shoulder, the severed end of the spike firmly in his hand. Edward saw something else, too—winding roots coiled around Russell's arm and extending out to snake down the length of the spike. That was what had halted its momentum.

From Russell's hand, the roots traveled down his arm and back down into the ground under the ripped-up floor. The signature of alchemy was obvious. Russell shook out his hand, and the roots crumbled and fell away.

"I-impossible!" Mugear gasped. "You have another Stone!?"

Russell raised both hands. They were empty, but in each palm was drawn an intricate transmutation circle.

"B-but how . . . ?" Mugear stammered.

Edward stared at Russell, his eyes wide. "You can use alchemy naturally?"

"I consider myself a third-grade alchemist at best, but, yes, I can."

"No, I've seen your research notes. You know more than you let on. I suspected as much at first . . . But when I saw you using the Stone, I thought you were relying on it because you had no power of your own."

It had taken split-second judgment and reflexes to stop that spike. It was clear that Russell possessed incredible raw talent. He might even be Edward's equal.

"I never used my alchemy, because I knew it would upset my father. I started using it again when I came here, but I still had my reservations. So I decided on a compromise. I would use alchemy, but only through the trial Stones I made. That way, I could still do research and hopefully help the town without really going back on my promise to my father . . . Or that's what I told myself, anyway. In the end, it was alchemy all the same, but I needed that excuse to keep going."

Russell spoke in a calm tone. "Now I realize it's all right for me to use alchemy. I never understood why he wanted me to quit—especially since you can do so much good with it." Russell's expression brightened. The sorrow that had shadowed his face had lifted. "I've decided I *will* use alchemy—as long as it helps others."

"So I'm the first to benefit from your change of heart, huh?" Edward laughed.

"I guess so!"

The boys smiled at each other.

"You think you can beat me without a Stone!?" howled Mugear.

Russell was unperturbed. "Of course. All you have is the Stone. Once we get into close range, it's all over for you."

Edward shook his head with a sigh. "You know, Russell, even though you're using your powers for good now, you're still pretty arrogant."

Russell nodded. "Get ready. He's coming."

"Huh?"

Mugear charged, firing his cannon straight at them.

"Whoa!" Edward dropped down and the bullet streaked through the air right above his head.

He felt Russell's foot tap his shoulder. "Well, what are you waiting for? Go get him."

"What? You want me to go at him alone?" Edward asked.

"Well, obviously you won't be able to close the distance between you with just alchemy. So why don't you worry about getting to him, and I'll worry about covering you on the way there. I'm better at defense, anyway."

As he spoke, light streaked from his hand along the torn-up floor and the roots beneath came alive, snaking and twisting through the cracks and crevices. Russell's technique was similar to the one used in alchemical medicine, only instead of manipulating human cells, he was manipulating the cells of plants.

Edward had his hands full before just holding off Mugear's attacks, but with Russell's help, the tables had definitely turned in his favor. Where Edward's attempts to dodge and cut Mugear's spikes in half had failed, Russell's strategy of containment and defense seemed to be working.

"Right, well . . . make sure you keep an eye on me," Edward said.

"Good luck. Put him in his place."

The two locked eyes and nodded. With that signal, they turned as one to the half-shattered wall Edward had thrown up in defense and pushed it over.

"There you are!" shouted Mugear, firing at Edward. "Come and get me!"

Russell's hands found a root stretching beneath the floor. The root bucked wildly, and innumerable tendrils shot into the air, catching the bullet and stopping it dead, midway to its mark. Mugear fired wildly. The shots were all blocked by flailing roots. The hall shook with the boom of cannon fire and the writhing of roots under the floor. The cacophony reached its peak, and a great cloud of plaster dust rose in the middle of the room. Edward hurtled out of the cloud above Mugear.

"Gotcha!"

Before Mugear could raise his weapon, Edward's sword came down, cutting his cannon clean in two. And before the pieces hit the ground, Mugear was out cold, knocked unconscious by a well-aimed punch to the side of the head.

Only when the guards dragged Mugear out the front gate did he discover that, while he had been fighting Edward and Russell, the two younger brothers had set fire to his alchemical laboratory and burned it to the ground.

"BEAUTIFUL, isn't it?" At sunset that evening, Edward watched shafts of light slanting over the outskirts of the town. The wind wasn't blowing, and the sky was clear. The late-day sun glimmered in the clear air.

"It'll be even more beautiful soon," Russell said. He sat down next to Edward. From their vantage point, they could see a single set of rails leading back into the town behind them. Edward and Alphonse were back where they started. This time, they were walking away from Xenotime and returning to the station. Russell and Fletcher had come to see them off.

On behalf of the townspeople, Belsio had apologized to the Elric brothers. "Don't worry about it, it was all their fault," Edward replied, grinning and pointing at Russell and Fletcher.

"Hey, we apologized!"

"Not enough!"

Russell scowled. He had apologized dozens of times, but it would never be enough for Edward. Impersonation was a serious enough crime to land Russell and Fletcher in jail, but neither Edward nor Alphonse wanted to take matters that far. In lieu of punishment, Edward had appointed Russell his personal masseuse and luggage porter.

"Are you sure you're okay? We could speak to the townspeople on your behalf," Edward offered, flashing Russell a look of concern. The townspeople were furious over the Tringum brothers' deception. Who knew what they would do to them when they got back to town? But to Russell's credit, he didn't seem afraid to face them.

"I'll take what's coming to me. Everything has to start from there."

"You too, Fletcher?" Alphonse asked.

Fletcher nodded. "I'm going to stick with my brother.

It's just the two of us now, and I've got to watch out for him . . . But I think he's doing the right thing . . . *this time.*" He gave his brother a little grin. Russell's face remained set and determined, but he didn't look unhappy.

Even when Russell had heard the truth about his father's disappearance, he held his emotions in check. He just put his arm around Fletcher's shoulder and said it was only what they had suspected all along.

Then he thanked Edward for all that he had done for them. Edward protested, "Stop that! It feels weird having you thank me!"

"Oh, so you'd rather I tell you what I really think of your alchemy powers?" Russell scowled.

Edward squinted up at Russell. "You putting me down?"

"'Putting you down'? You already *are* . . ." Russell replied, standing on his tiptoes for effect.

"Ha! You're still a jerk, after all."

NOT FAR from the bickering older brothers, Alphonse was saying his farewells to Belsio, who had accompanied them to the edge of town. "Thanks for all your help, Mr. Belsio."

"Come visit us again sometime soon. I just hope we'll be able to offer you a little more hospitality next time."

The town had been in an uproar since the authorities dragged Mugear off to jail. Lemac had been the first to organize the disillusioned townspeople, proposing a town meeting to decide how to allocate the remaining research money and what their next move should be. Belsio was in charge of the town's field restoration project, and Delfino was in charge of organizing the goldsmiths who remained. Everyone had something to do. It was the start of a new era.

Fletcher held his hand out to Alphonse. "Thank you." It was Alphonse who had given him the courage to stand up to his brother, and Fletcher knew he would never be the same. "I'll keep at it until Russell relies on me as much as Edward relies on you, Alphonse."

"I just hope he doesn't only rely on you to buy him bandages!"

"I just hope he keeps himself out of fights."

The two smiled at each other. Beside them, the older brothers had finally stopped trading insults. Russell handed the traveling trunk back to Edward.

"Thank you. Really."

Edward grabbed the hand Russell extended and gave it a firm shake. "Good luck. You know, if you wanted to, you could probably become a State Alchemist. You're good enough to pass the exams in a heartbeat. Oh, but that attitude of yours might be a problem."

"Really?" Russell said. "It didn't seem to be a roadblock for you."

"Yeah, yeah . . ." Edward grinned.

Now that they had finished putting each other down, they both felt sad that they had to part. The setting sun painted the land around them a deep red.

"Well, take care. I hope you find what you're looking for."

"Thanks. You too."

With that, the real Elric brothers left Xenotime and their new friends behind them. The Tringum brothers turned around and headed back down the railway, their true names restored. And so ended the incident of Xenotime's impostor alchemists.

ON THEIR WAY back to town, Russell and Fletcher stopped in front of one of the trees Belsio had planted. It looked frail and thin against the darkening evening sky, but Russell said in time it would grow tall and bear fruit.

"Are you sure?" Fletcher asked.

Russell nodded and withdrew a flask from his back pocket. Inside, a few drops of crimson fluid sloshed, reflecting the light of the setting sun and glowing brighter than ever before.

Russell unstoppered the flask, bent over, and poured the liquid by the base of the tree. The Water that had meant so much to them for so long disappeared into the parched soil. They looked up at the tree, but nothing happened. It was as though the tree and the Water were telling them that all the work they had done, all of their effort, was to no avail.

Russell straightened up. The chains around him were finally gone for good.

"Let's go," he said. He glanced at his little brother.

"Yeah, let's go."

They draped their arms around each other's shoulders and walked the last stretch to town. The future they walked toward was uncertain, but it was a future they were choosing for themselves.

Epilogue

THE RAILWAY STATION was illuminated by the pale light of the moon by the time Edward and Alphonse arrived, but they were in time to catch the last train out. They stepped into an empty railcar and sat down across from each other. Edward quickly spread out, lying down on his side.

"I hope they'll be okay," Alphonse muttered to himself.

The Tringum brothers had lied to the whole town, and they were sure to be punished. Even though they deserved what was coming to them, Alphonse couldn't help but feel sorry for them.

"They'll be fine," Edward reassured him. "You saw the look on their faces. They were ready for anything. They'll pay their dues and move on."

Alphonse breathed a little easier. "You're right. You know, I didn't notice it at first, but once Russell made up his mind to come clean, I saw something in his face that reminded me of you."

No matter what, Edward always had an aura of absolute

self-confidence. Alphonse had seen that same gleam in Russell's eyes when they parted. Now that he thought about it, Edward and Russell were alike in a number of ways. They had similar builds, they both had younger brothers, they shared an affinity for alchemy, and their smiles were undaunted.

"Fletcher reminds me of you, too, Al."

"Huh? Am I really that . . . innocent?"

"No, not like that. I mean, I look at him and I realize how hard it must be to have such a jerk for an older brother."

"So you admit you're a jerk?"

The two caught each other's eye and burst out laughing.

"I hope we get to see them again sometime, Ed."

"Yeah. That Russell was an impressive alchemist. I'm sure I'll hear his name again someday."

"He was that good?"

"Absolutely. If we had gone at it for real, I'm not sure I would have made it out of that place in one piece. By the time he's famous, hopefully we'll both be back in our original bodies," Edward added quietly.

They had failed to get any further in their quest for the secret of the Philosopher's Stone, but there were many places left to explore. Their journey would continue.

"We'll keep trying," Alphonse said.

"Yeah."

Alphonse nodded and turned away to open the small

paper bag he was holding in his hand. Fletcher had given it to him when they parted. Inside, Fletcher had told him, were two things to aid them on their journey. "Look," Alphonse said, holding up the bag so Edward could see. "Poultices and medicine. We'll be okay if you get in trouble again." Alphonse shook the bag. "Oh, wait. There's something else."

Alphonse turned the bag upside down, and a piece of paper fell out.

"A letter! It's for you—from Russell."

"Aw, it's probably just one last parting jibe," Edward waved his hand dismissively at Alphonse. "Go ahead, read it."

"Okay." Alphonse unfolded the paper and began to read. "Dear Edward, I owe you one more apology. The truth is, I was lying about my age."

"See? I told you!" Edward shouted, bolting upright. "I knew there was no way he could be my age and be that tall!" He was ecstatic.

Alphonse looked down at the letter, then up at his brother. Then he folded the letter together.

"So, how old is he? I'm betting nineteen! When I'm nineteen, I'll be even taller!"

"I'm sure you're right," Alphonse said quietly, turning to gaze out at the moonlit landscape racing by.

Edward poked Alphonse from across the aisle. "That wasn't it, was it? Come on, how old is he?"

"He didn't say. That's all he wrote."

"Really?" Edward grinned, convinced Alphonse was just giving him a hard time. "Come on! What's the big deal?" He reached out toward Alphonse's pocket.

Alphonse shied away, but Edward grabbed him and tried to take the letter.

"Ed, knock it off!"

"C'mon, Al, what's there to hide?" He snatched the letter out of Alphonse's grasp. "Got it! I can't believe you wouldn't give it to me. You're such a kid sometimes."

Edward opened the letter and darted away from Alphonse, who made a feeble attempt to get it back. Edward stood in the middle of the railcar grinning broadly. "I knew I'd find out how old he was in the end!" Edward chuckled as he began to read the letter, then suddenly froze.

"No-o-o-o-o-o-o!"

Edward's scream echoed through the railcar. Alphonse sighed and put his head in his hands.

Dear Edward,
I owe you one more apology. The truth is, I was lying about my age. I'm really only 14, a year younger than you. Sorry I lied.
Regards,
Russell Tringum

Bonus Story

The Phantom
of Warehouse 13

The time: High noon.
The place: Eastern Command HQ.

"Warehouse 13?"

Two lacquer-black eyes blinked suspiciously from beneath a shock of hair. The man who spoke was Colonel Roy Mustang, the Fire Alchemist, and chief officer of Eastern Command. He lifted his eyes from his documents to look at Second Lieutenant Jean Havoc standing in front of his desk, nodding his head enthusiastically, a cigarette dangling from his mouth.

"What are you talking about?" Roy asked. "We have only twelve numbered warehouses in Eastern Command."

He glanced out his office window. He could see all the warehouses on the base from here. He counted twelve warehouses in a row, aligned perpendicular to his line of sight. At the far end sat three more warehouses, marked with the letters "A," "B," and "C."

"You're forgetting one more," said Havoc, raising a finger. "Warehouse 13, in other words . . . Aren't you interested?"

Jean Havoc was the sort of fellow who struck people as *odd* at first glance. He always did good, skilled work, but his attitude was abysmal. Regardless of whether he stood before an officer or a Master Sergeant, he always held that cigarette in his mouth. When people protested, he wouldn't even respond, swinging general opinion against him even further. He merely let the comments wash over him. He was slippery that way. No matter what reprimand or complaint was made, nothing seemed to stick.

In an unusual display of consideration, Havoc poured Roy a cup of coffee, and then, sipping at his own cup, he pulled up a chair and began to smoke. Roy didn't bother reprimanding him for smoking in his office. After all, he wasn't exactly being a model officer himself, wasting time with this ridiculous banter. Pointing a finger at Havoc would merely be pointing a finger back at himself.

"So what if there is a Warehouse 13? Is that a problem?" Roy's tone of voice and disinterested expression made his disdain for the topic clear. The sooner Havoc agreed it was ridiculous and left him alone, the better.

Across the desk, Havoc knew quite well that his story gave

Col. Mustang a much-desired opportunity to waste time. So, he sat back in his chair and slowly sipped his coffee. "Oh, there's a big problem."

"Explain."

"Well . . . if you pass by this Warehouse 13 in the middle of the night, you hear sounds, noises—someone weeping, someone digging in the dirt."

"What is this, some kind of ghost story?" Roy scowled and turned his gaze back to his documents.

"Not fond of ghost stories, Colonel?"

Roy glared at the thinly veiled challenge in Havoc's voice. "I'm not scared."

"Oh, that's too bad." Havoc seemed deflated, deprived of a chance to scare his superior officer.

"There's nothing 'too bad' about it!" Roy put his hands on his temples. "Alchemy is a science. We must strive to be logical in all things. I suppose that's why I've never been one for ghost stories."

"Quite the opposite for me, I'm afraid," said Havoc. "I love a good ghost story. Can't help but tell them, in fact."

Havoc sighed.

"I've found that most scary things, when you take a good look at them, turn out to be nothing much at all." Roy looked up at the window and waved Havoc over with his hand. "Look," he said, pointing. "There's your Warehouse 13."

Havoc looked down the row of numbered warehouses,

his eyes eventually coming to rest on the three warehouses facing them at the far end.

"See those lettered warehouses? There's your Warehouse 13."

Havoc gave Roy a perplexed look.

"Picture a moonless night. You're walking down the row of warehouses, and when you get to the end, you look up . . . at Warehouse B."

"Oh, I get it," said Havoc. "If it were dark enough and you were scared enough, that 'B' would look like a '13.'"

"And the weeping sound was just the blowing of the wind, no doubt," said Roy, satisfied. "The night can make you see and hear things that aren't there. Besides, there's nothing to be scared of, Warehouse 13 or no. If there's a ghost out there, he's trespassing on military property. You go out there with that attitude, and nothing can touch you. The only reason people get scared is because they *expect* to be scared." Roy's voice rang with the authority of a true commanding officer.

Havoc nodded and smiled. "Well said, sir. That makes perfect sense to me—look at things with a fearful mind, and of course you'll be frightened!"

"So, who is it that's been spreading this ghost story around, anyway?" asked Roy. "Someone who jumps at every shadow doesn't belong in my unit. I'll go tell him that his ghost is just some dry bush out there whistling in the wind."

"Maybe you could say something, sir? Please, it would be

good for morale. Everyone's jumpy enough as it is. Ah, and it's almost time for lunch."

"That late already?"

The time had flown. If Captain Hawkeye saw them wasting time like this, she'd be furious, but she was off base today. Hence the leisurely pace. The two made their way down the hall toward the central room where the whole base crew would be gathered. There were no emergencies of note, and things were lazy, so they all took advantage of the relaxed schedule to eat lunch together and shoot the breeze. Roy looked out through the large windows that lined the hallway to the central green, where a black and white dog frolicked in the grass.

"Look, it's Capt. Hawkeye's dog."

The dog was still only a puppy. Master Sergeant Fuery had brought it in one day, even though pets were forbidden in the base dormitory. Hawkeye had admonished him, but they couldn't find anyone to take care of the dog. Unwilling to get rid of the dog, Hawkeye eventually took it in herself.

"Be warned: I'm a cruel mistress," she had said as she picked the dog up in her arms, and M.Sgt. Fuery began to weep. The general opinion was that he had started crying because he was so happy that someone had taken in the dog, and they wouldn't have to get rid of him. However, some people whispered that it was the rare sight of Capt. Hawkeye smiling that had moved him to tears.

Soon after, Capt. Hawkeye declared that she would spend time with the dog as part of an experiment in training animals for military service. Though she hadn't wanted it on base, claiming a "mixing of public and Master Sergeant concerns," Roy had said he didn't care, and now the dog was sure to be at the base on days like today, when work was slow. Whenever Hawkeye had an early shift or late shift, or spent the night, the dog would run freely on the grounds.

"I suppose it could be a watchdog," said Roy. When they were looking for someone to take care of the dog, Roy was one of the first ones declared unfit for the task.

"Look at him playing out there, so innocent," said Havoc, standing next to Roy. Havoc was the second to be deemed unfit for dog-sitting. Something about an offhand remark he had made about dogs "going well with gravy." He had been joking, of course, but he had said it with such a serious look on his face that no one trusted him with the dog after that. Even now, weeks later, Fuery refused to leave the dog alone with Havoc for any length of time.

"I'm hungry," said Havoc suddenly. "Let's eat."

Maybe his stomach had growled because it was lunchtime, or maybe it was because he saw the dog. Had Fuery been there to hear him, he surely would have assumed the latter, grabbed the dog, and run several kilometers before stopping. Havoc had earned a bit of a reputation for his poorly timed comments.

The dog had grown since the day it joined them on the base, and these days it was more playful than ever. It ran around the central courtyard in endless circles.

"Well? Has it become the ultimate loyal, unwavering hound? Forever in perfect harmony with its master?" asked Havoc.

"Not yet, though he does shake without me asking now." Roy held his hand out to the dog. The dog gave him a perplexed look and sat perfectly still, like always. Roy had been clear up front about his preference in dogs: faithful, diligent, hardworking. But there was something in his face that said what he really wanted was someone to do all his work for him, so he could live a life of ease. This contributed greatly to the decision to remove Roy from the list of possible candidates to care for the dog.

"He'll need a little more training before he can sign papers for me," said Roy glumly.

"You'll be waiting your whole life for that," said Havoc, promptly dashing his hopes.

The two had reached the door to the main hall. Roy grabbed the handle and opened the door with a click. On the other side, he was greeted by a loud voice.

"Everyone, rejoice! The colonel has decided to lead tonight's mission!"

With a start, Roy realized it was Havoc. He had snuck past him when he opened the door and now held the door wide open for the unwitting Roy.

"Huh? What's this now?" Things were happening too fast for Roy to understand what was going on, but when he saw everyone standing in the lunchroom, sandwiches clutched in one hand, eyes looking at him expectantly, he knew something was up.

"I wouldn't be frightened of any ghosts if the colonel came with us!" said Falman. Falman was warrant officer on the base—a scrawny fellow with squinty eyes that now shone in Roy's direction.

"The more people, the better!" said Breda. Like Havoc, Heymans Breda was a second lieutenant, and he was Falman's direct opposite. He was as brawny as they came and looked like the last person in the room who would need the colonel's help for anything, least of all a ghost.

"Colonel! Please do something! I can't go out at night, I'm so scared!" said M.Sgt. Fuery, running over to cling to Roy's sleeve. He was on the verge of tears. Fuery was a serious-looking young fellow with short black hair and large glasses. He looked even younger than his already young age. He was often mistaken for a junior high student.

Roy still had no idea what was going on, but he didn't like it. Pulling his arm out of Fuery's grasp, he whirled to confront Havoc. "What do you mean 'tonight's mission'? What's going on here?"

"Why, whatever do you mean? It's what we were just

talking about! The Eastern Command Haunting, sir! Didn't you say you'd help find out the truth?"

"Huh?"

Indeed, Roy had claimed he would prove that this ghost was nothing more than the product of idle fears, but that had been a casual conversation. He had never imagined that Havoc might twist it into an offer to lead some harebrained spook chase.

"Well, no . . . I said I'd tell the truth to whoever was spreading this rumor, but I didn't say a thing about any mission!"

"You mean . . . you aren't going to help us out?" asked Fuery, worry in his eyes. Fuery's hands were quaking. He looked miserable. Roy realized he had to do something.

"Well, it's not that I won't help . . . It's just, this mission, I . . . " Roy didn't want to just say 'yes' and commit himself to this scheme.

"It's okay, M.Sgt. Fuery," said Havoc. "It's not you. He's this mean to everyone."

Havoc laughed and Roy steamed.

"Look who's talking! And here I thought you'd just come to my office to waste time telling ghost stories!"

Havoc raised his hands to the sky in a mock prayer for pity. "What are you saying? Me? Waste time? I lead a life of utmost diligence!"

"Liar," Roy spat, but Havoc wasn't listening.

Havoc pulled out a chair for the colonel and spread a map of the base grounds on the table. "Okay, mission leader. Let's get all the details straight."

"Who are you calling 'mission leader,' and what's all this about a 'mission' anyway?"

"Why, our mission to reveal the truth behind this haunting! I'm the strategist, and you're our leader!" he said, pointing at Roy.

Roy knocked his hand aside.

Breda stepped over and ran his hand over the map, counting out the warehouses. "Here are the numbered warehouses, one through twelve, and then there's one more—"

Before Breda could point out the non-existent Warehouse 13, Roy grabbed his hand.

"Here's your Warehouse 13," he said, pointing at Warehouse B. "The truth has been revealed! Our mission is a success!"

He stood up triumphantly, but Havoc put a hand on his shoulder.

"We're not letting you get out of this, Colonel. We're really scared, and we really need you to do something about it."

"You just want one more person for your group so you can throw me at the ghost first."

"Of course we do! We need as many people as we can get. Strength in numbers, and all that."

Havoc's voice was as jovial as always, but his eyes looked unusually serious. Roy realized that with Fuery on the verge of tears and even Breda looking pale, he wouldn't be able to let the subject slide. He didn't want to get involved, but he had no choice.

"Fine," said Roy, sighing as he sat back down in his chair. "Tell me what happened. From the beginning."

The first mention of something odd going on at Eastern Command had come almost a month before. Falman heard it first. Someone from town told him about it when he was out on a shopping mission.

"You've been busy nights at the Command Center, haven't you?" they had said. Falman had brushed it off as small talk. But five minutes later, another person said almost exactly the same thing. When he asked why, he learned that people had heard digging noises from the base. They assumed it was some kind of official project. He inquired further and unleashed a flood of reports and speculation.

"I heard digging sounds there the other night."

"It sounds like one person digging . . . but why would they dig at night, with no lights?"

"The guards say no one on base has been working nights outside . . ."

"But nobody who's not in the military is allowed on base . . ."

"Maybe it's not a person at all!"

"Maybe it's a ghost!"

"Didn't the base used to be a prison?"

"They executed people there!"

"Eastern Command is haunted!"

"The ghost wanders the base at night, looking for unwitting souls to eat!"

The rumors grew and grew.

Roy laughed. "This is ridiculous. This is nothing but rumors feeding rumors until they got out of control."

But no one in the room was smiling. Roy looked around. Fuery and Falman, in particular, seemed grim. They were looking down at the lunch table with pale faces.

"What?" asked Roy. "Don't tell me you heard it too?"

The two nodded. Falman was the first to break the resulting silence. "We pass by the warehouses on our way to the dormitory. Just the other night, I had to make that walk after my shift let out. I'd heard the rumors, and that got me thinking about the warehouses. I walked quietly and then—"

"You heard it?"

"Someone digging . . . scraping in the ground." Falman gulped and turned even paler.

"You too, M.Sgt. Fuery?"

Fuery nodded. "On my way back to the dormitory at night. But . . . " Fuery's voice was trembling and goose bumps appeared on his arms. "I heard weeping." Fuery screwed his eyes shut, as though he didn't want to remember it.

"...Weeping?" Roy thought it must have been the wind, a trick of the ears, but he couldn't just outright deny what Fuery was saying.

"So, how far has the rumor gotten in town?" he asked at last.

"Well, here's the story right now: There used to be a Warehouse 13 in Eastern Command. A woman died there long ago, which is why the warehouse was destroyed, and her remains along with it. Now she comes back at night, searching for her bones."

"That's quite the story to get from some overheard digging noises," said Roy, impressed.

"Please," said Fuery, "you have to do something. I'm too scared to go to the dormitory."

Roy was at a loss.

"Was there ever really a Warehouse 13?" asked Breda.

"Not that I know of," said Roy. "Though I do know that the three lettered warehouses were built first. The numbered warehouses were built later, all at once, to meet storage needs during the civil war. So, there was never a space at the end of the numbered warehouses for a thirteenth."

"So Warehouse 13 is probably Warehouse B after all."

"That's what I think...but I don't know about this digging and weeping," said Roy. "Has anyone gone to check it out?"

"Why, that's what we're going to do tonight!" said Havoc. "You've got a late shift—just stay a little later and do some overtime." He was already checking work schedules.

"At night?" asked Roy incredulously. "You're going at night?"

Roy had said that ghost stories didn't bother him, but after hearing Falman and Fuery's accounts of the sounds they had heard, he began to feel a little nervous. "Why not just go now?"

"Because the ghost comes out at night!" said Havoc. "We won't find anything if we go out now! The Eastern Command Paranormal Investigation Squad leaves from here at 0100 hours sharp."

"Wait, we can't just do stuff like this on base! If we get caught . . ."

Roy didn't have to tell Havoc who would get mad if she found them running about like school kids in the dark.

"Capt. Hawkeye gets off early tonight. We'll be fine."

"Yes, but . . ." Roy felt less and less enthusiastic about going out at night to the very spot of the rumored haunting. Plus, it was starting to sound like a pain in the rear. "One in the morning? This weeping's probably just the wind blowing through some cracks in the warehouse siding."

Havoc was not to be dissuaded. "Colonel, your men are frightened! Are you just going to let them be? Your poor, poor men . . ."

"Bah," said Roy. "You just want to get me involved in your little farce."

"Oh, I didn't want to go either, but when M.Sgt. Fuery came to me, well, I knew it was time to pluck up my courage and do the right thing," said Havoc.

"Me too."

"Same here."

"And I did hear the digging too, after all . . ."

M.Sgt. Fuery must have been truly frightened. He had gone crying to everybody. He looked up at Roy now, and his eyes were watery with tears. "Please . . . please don't leave us! I'm so scared."

I really don't want to go, thought Roy, but he couldn't figure out how to say it.

"Colonel!!"

A few moments later, Fuery was hanging on his arm, pleading with him to go.

"All right! All right, I'll go!" said Roy. He sighed and looked down at the map of the base.

IT WAS ONE O'CLOCK in the morning. Roy had finished killing time under the pretext of working late and began walking the hallway down to the central room. Falman and Havoc were on shift, and Fuery and Breda had been wasting time like Roy.

"What a pain."

Roy had finally given up trying to get out of the mission. It was the only way to settle this matter once and for all. Roy thought about his men. Poor M.Sgt. Fuery was so scared of the ghost he couldn't go back to his dormitory, but even he agreed to join the mission. It was either that or wait in the lunchroom by himself, and that was no option with a ghost about. He had asked Hawkeye for permission to keep the dog on base. Roy figured he'd probably be clinging to the poor pooch for dear life until the mission started.

Falman, who had heard the ghost digging, wanted the mystery solved as well. Breda was joining just to say he had, and as for Havoc, he said he was scared, but no doubt this was all just an excuse for him to have fun running around at night without getting in trouble.

"If you let this slide, it'll definitely have a negative effect on morale, Colonel . . ."

Not to mention that if word of the rumor reached Central Command, they'd definitely get a reprimand. Worse, Roy knew the officer in charge at Central, and there was a better than good chance that he'd take a personal interest in their rumor for one of his publicity schemes. Eastern Command would become an entertainment facility—a tourist destination for boggle-eyed recruits to come see the famous haunted warehouse—and Roy had no intention of letting his base become a fairground. He decided that it was in his best interest to get to the bottom of this rumor and resolve the whole situation quietly.

"It's tough being a mid-level manager," he grumbled as he came to a stop before the door to the main hall. He would clean this matter up quickly and quietly, so that no one at the top would hear so much as a whisper about it. Roy reached out to open the door, and his eyes opened wide.

"What's this?"

Someone had pasted a giant piece of paper on the door to the main room. In giant letters, it read:

Eastern Command
Paranormal Investigation HQ

Roy ripped the sign off the door and stormed into the room, the tattered paper clutched in his hand. "Don't hang up this crap! What if somebody important saw this?"

"Aw, and I just finished making that," said Havoc, woefully collecting the ripped bits of paper that had fallen.

"Stop making this a bigger deal than it has to be!"

"Now, now, sir," said Havoc. Havoc tried to calm Roy down, while Breda and Falman busied themselves with pieces of bread on the table next to him.

"We'll need two more pieces," said Breda. "And more sausages. Then when M.Sgt. Fuery gets here, we'll be ready to go."

"Why are you making lunch bags?" Roy stared at the two, dumbfounded.

"Why, if we're going on a field trip, we've got to have some fun!" said Havoc, innocently.

"Here's your midnight snack, Colonel." Breda walked up and handed the colonel a small brown paper bag. Roy's hand shook with rage.

"Look, I'm only going out here because I don't want to see Eastern Command turn into some kind of tourist destination. And I don't want everyone here to get a *severe* drop in pay because high command has to do an investigation of us. This is no field trip, so don't make it one."

"Colonel, it's just that Fuery was so scared, we thought we'd try to lighten things up a little. Wiener?"

Havoc held out a small luncheon sausage to Roy. Roy scowled. "We don't need lunches!"

Havoc put a hand on his forehead in mock pain. "Oh, to see our poor master sergeant in such distress . . ."

"Stop pretending to be concerned."

"You could tell?"

As Roy and Havoc were exchanging barbs, Fuery arrived. He didn't so much as look up at the other people in the room, and his face was as pale and quiet as that of a prisoner on death row. Every motion he made seemed to scream *I don't want to go*. He looked much worse off than he had at noon.

"Here, I made you a midnight snack," said Falman, handing the quaking master sergeant a lunch bag in an attempt to cheer him up.

"Th-thank you." Fuery grabbed the bag tightly, like a man

accepting his last supper, and held it in his arms. "I-I'm not going to run away or anything, b-but I'm so scared."

"Don't worry," said Breda, gently. "There's really no such thing as ghosts. And besides, we'll be next to you the whole way."

"B-Breda . . ." Fuery's eyes filled with tears, and he went to hug the second lieutenant. "Thaaank yooooou!"

"Whoa! Hey!" said Breda, running off to the far side of the room. "Keep those dog-touching hands of yours away from me!" Breda was far more scared of dog hairs than ghosts, it seemed.

Roy tapped Fuery's shoulder. "M.Sgt. Fuery, really, there's no need to be frightened. We'll get to the bottom of this, and you'll see that it was nothing all along. The weeping you think you heard was most likely wind through some building materials piled up in one of those warehouses. I'm sure of it. There's no such thing as ghosts."

"Th-thank you, Colonel." Fuery seemed a bit more at ease.

"Well, shall we go?" said Havoc, eagerness evident in his voice. "Our first encounter with a real ghost!"

With those words, M.Sgt. Fuery's newfound ease disappeared in an instant. Second Lt. Havoc truly excelled at saying the wrong thing at the wrong time.

WHEN THEY OPENED THE DOOR to the outside, a strong, chill wind blew in their faces, making the warmth of the day seem like nothing but a figment of their imagination.

"Nasty weather," muttered Roy. The moon lay hidden behind dark clouds, and the sky was a sullen black. They looked up at the dark silhouettes of the warehouses that Roy had looked down on from his office. Falman closed the door behind them with a loud click, and the light from the room was cut off. The darkness around them grew deeper. Everyone had wanted to get this over with and maybe to tell a joke or two to lighten things up, but now that the task was before them, no one wanted to go. Huddling together, they slowly made their way down off of the main hall's patio and onto the unpaved dirt road that led down the line of warehouses.

"Stop pushing!" said Roy. The others were crowding behind him, pushing him to the front of the line.

"Sorry, just didn't want to walk in front of a ranking officer," said Havoc, crouching behind Roy and using him as a human shield against the terrors of the night.

"I'm scared, I'm scared," whispered Fuery.

"You're only scared because you think there's something to be scared of," said Falman in a cold, calculating voice from where he was hiding behind Roy's back.

Breda made the suggestion that they sing something. They were all trying unsuccessfully to hide the fear that had snuck into their very hearts, leaving them cold and shaking.

"Eeeek!" Breda shrieked suddenly, and everyone's stomach jumped through his throat.

"What? What is it?"

"Ow!"

"Is something there?"

"Who stepped on my foot?"

One scream had set them all off, and now they were jumping like a pack of nervous animals. Only a few moments had passed since they stepped outside, and already, the fear was an epidemic. The only one even slightly calm was Roy, and so it fell to him to get everyone else back in line. Breda's shriek had panicked him for a moment, but the boot coming down on his foot brought him painfully back to his senses. "Second Lieutenant Havoc, your foot."

"Oh, sorry, sir."

"Why was your foot all the way over here?"

"Accident, sir."

"What's going on here? Breda, what was that scream about?"

"Nooo . . . keep it away!" said Breda. "Bad dog! Stay back!"

The black-and-white puppy was nipping at Breda's feet. Everyone breathed a sigh of relief.

Fuery smiled. "What's wrong, boy? Want to come with us? Colonel, can we take him?"

Before Fuery could finish, Breda shouted from behind Roy and Havoc, whom he was using as a shield against the dog. "No! No way!"

"But . . . he says he's lonely."

"Don't interpret for the dog!" cried Breda. "No, no, no!"

"M.Sgt. Fuery, tie up the dog and come along," ordered Roy. Sullenly, Fuery nodded and went back to tie up the dog outside the main hall. Now that everyone had calmed down, they began to walk again. Now they could hear the dog, tied up, howling behind them. They all froze. The one success of Hawkeye's training had been to keep the dog from barking. Now it rarely made a noise without reason.

"Quiet down!" hissed Fuery back at the dog.

"Did you feed him?" asked Roy. "Maybe he's hungry."

"No, I fed him—and he's never howled like that before when he wanted food. Maybe he's lonely after all . . ."

"No, that's not it," said Havoc. "Haven't you ever heard that dogs have the power to sense the supernatural? Some people say they can even sense the future . . ."

"I've heard dogs bark when their owner is in danger," noted Roy.

"That's it. Soon, something horrible is going to happen to one of us. That's what the dog is saying. He's close to M.Sgt. Fuery. He must be trying to warn him of danger."

"Are you trying to scare us?" said Roy, scowling, but it was too late. The nervous tension that had left them momentarily when the dog first arrived now came back with a vengeance.

"Are we going to be okay?" Falman asked, pointing up. They had just arrived at the first warehouse, and its silhouette stood pitch black against the sky. They were all wondering the same thing.

"We'll be fine," said Roy. "The dog's probably wrong, anyway."

"Bah," said Breda. "How is a creature that can't even control its own saliva supposed to predict the future? It's baloney, pure and simple."

Unconvinced, Fuery looked up into the darkness, trembling. "What's out there . . . ?" he said quietly.

Everyone fell silent. The warehouses were lined up along the left side of the wide path along which they walked. Other buildings lined the right, a good distance away from the warehouses. The light from the building they had left barely lit their way now, and the darkness grew even deeper ahead.

Like a virus, Fuery's fear had begun to spread and infect the others, starting with Roy, whose sleeve he clutched, then moving on to Havoc cowering behind them and Breda and Falman behind him. All of them walked in a huddle, with nervous little steps, trying to hide behind Roy's back in the growing darkness.

"Why do I have to be in the lead?"

"Ranking officers first, sir," said Havoc gently, but the hand he put on Roy's shoulder to push him forward remained firm.

"Why is this the only time rank seems to matter around here?" grumbled Roy.

Havoc's reasons for dragging Roy along on this crazy

mission were becoming all too clear. Without him here, either Havoc or Breda would be the one in front. It grew darker around them as they passed the first warehouse, then the second, and by the time they reached the fourth warehouse, they couldn't see a thing, even though their eyes had grown accustomed to the dark.

"Anyone bring a light?"

"Oh, yeah," said Falman, bringing out an old lantern. Havoc lit the wick. The flickering yellow-orange light spread from the lantern, a diffuse glow in the darkness. After a brief silence, Falman muttered, "For some reason, that makes me even more frightened."

The lamp was a classic box-shaped lantern, and despite its glass windows, every time the wind blew, the flame would shake. The shimmering orange light made their shadows leap and quiver in a terrifying dance on the warehouse walls.

"Well, we can't do anything about that. They're just our own shadows." Roy straightened up, and his shadow bent with a sudden gust of wind.

"Hey, you're right. Look at this." Falman held up his hands together in front of the lamp and made shadow puppets on the warehouse wall. "Look! A cute dog!" The dog-shaped shadow on the wall twisted in the flickering light.

"I appreciate the idea, but I'm afraid I have to ask you to stop, Falman," said Roy. The flickering flame had transformed Falman's shadow-dog into a writhing wolf with gaping, tooth-filled jaws.

"Let's keep going. At this pace, we'll never get there."

"Yeah. Let's get this over with so we can go back and drink some hot coffee."

Even though they'd stopped at every twitch of the lantern flame, they had reached Warehouse 6.

"What was in this warehouse?" asked Breda, holding up the lamp to see the number stenciled above the main door.

"Uh, well," began Roy, "these warehouses all hold desks and other materials like that, things we aren't currently using. Anything we're likely to run low on often, we put in Warehouse 1, less often in Warehouse 2, and so on. We hardly ever use Warehouse 6 and the others. They're mostly filled with odd parts and junk we never use but can't justify getting rid of. For all I know, there might not even be anything in there."

"You mean you've never seen inside?" asked Breda.

"Just once, when I first arrived on base."

"So you don't really know what's in this warehouse?" Those words, which normally would have been innocent enough, now sounded darkly ominous. Everyone gulped.

"What would we do if we heard someone scream from inside?" Breda joked, but his own fear echoed clearly in his voice, and it ended up sounding nothing like a joke at all. Everyone edged over to the right to get as far away from the warehouse as they could.

"You know, they say that ghosts like places where the air is stagnant, where no one's been for a long time," said Falman, half to break the nervous silence.

Now the idea had been planted in everyone's mind, as clear as scientific fact: a warehouse with stagnant air equals a warehouse with a ghost. Their footsteps became like those of cattle being led to the slaughter. At this pace, they would all catch cold before reaching their destination.

Roy sighed and walked up to the next warehouse in line, Warehouse 8. "Well, let's check it out. If we shine that lantern through the window, we should be able to see inside."

The other four pressed back against the wall of the building opposite, shaking their heads.

"No way!"

"No, please, no!"

"Colonel, please!"

Roy walked over and physically dragged them back toward the warehouse. They resisted him like children, digging their heels into the ground. "Listen," he said. "We're here to investigate the truth behind this 'Warehouse 13' and those digging sounds, but now we're so scared about what might be inside *this* warehouse that we can't go any farther. Let's just check out everything that scares us and get it taken care of."

"No!" said Fuery, shaking.

"Keep saying that, and you'll be too scared to get anything

out of the warehouse even if you have to for work. Look, I'm not coming out here on another one of these fact-finding missions. Let's get this over with tonight. Second Lt. Havoc, get M.Sgt. Fuery over here. Officer Falman, no running."

The four shuffled over reluctantly.

"Havoc, bring a stepladder. There's one over by Warehouse 6." Roy asked him because he seemed to be the least scared of the bunch, but Havoc refused immediately.

"No way, no, sir! I'm not going there by myself!"

"Very well, then," said Roy. "I'll go. You all wait here with Breda."

"No! Please don't leave us, Colonel!" moaned M.Sgt. Fuery.

"Please!" said Havoc.

"We need you!" said Falman.

Roy was unusually popular this evening. The three were grabbing on to him so tightly he could barely breathe. In the end, they found an empty crate by the warehouse wall they could stand on to see through the lowest window. All of them clambered up onto the crate and peered in through the window.

The inside was completely dark. They could faintly see the outline of a window on the other side of the warehouse.

"See? Look. No ghosts, and no screams." Roy was victorious, but by the time everyone had calmed down again, it was already past two o'clock in the morning.

"I THINK we've already gotten as scared as we possibly could. We'll be fine now no matter what happens," said Roy, biting into a sandwich. The five had decided it was time for an early morning snack, and so they sat down in a circle, in the middle of the path. In lieu of a campfire, they placed the lantern in the center of the circle; it was their only protection against the horrors that lurked in the cold night.

They were a giddy bunch, rejoicing in the respite from terror that the familiar sandwiches and warm soup gave them. Havoc nodded at Roy's words and bit into a wiener. "Yup, once you've hit the bottom, you can't go any deeper."

"So . . . we can't get any more scared than we are now?"

"That's right."

Not even Roy seemed willing to question the idea that fear could have some kind of limit.

"You know, I feel pretty good," said Falman.

"I'm fine, too!" said Fuery.

"All right, then, how about a ghost story?" said Havoc, grinning. They all laughed like they had a screw loose. It was Falman who stopped the laughter.

"Okay. Has anyone heard the story of the flower-seller's wife?"

As appropriate to someone telling a ghost story, Falman spoke in a low, quiet voice. Everyone fell silent.

"Once, there was a couple who ran a flower shop. They did good business, selling a variety of well-grown flowers to happy customers every day. But one day, the wife fell sick and died. The florist was very sad, and he put the flowers they had grown together at her grave. He realized then that, even though he sold flowers, he had never given flowers to his wife before that day. It was the least he could do, he thought, and he set her gravestone with a glorious selection of bouquets to honor her memory."

"That's a nice story."

"Yeah."

Everyone smiled, but Falman shook his head. "Wrong."

"Huh?"

"That night, the wife came to the flower-seller's bedside."

"To thank him?" asked Fuery.

"That's what he thought, too, but he was quite mistaken." As he got into the telling, Falman's voice had grown quite soft. Everyone leaned in to hear.

"The face of his wife as she stood at his bedside was filled with sadness. For you see, though they had lived together for so long, he had never given her flowers, and now, only when she was dead did he finally give her a bouquet."

"But . . . he did give her flowers! I mean, she couldn't be mad at him for that!" whispered Fuery.

"Yes, he gave her flowers . . . but not her favorite. He gave her the wrong kind!"

"W-what happened then?"

"On the next day and the next, the florist picked flowers and brought them to her grave, but the face of his wife grew more and more unhappy with each passing night. The florist had spoken with her many times about which flowers she preferred, but he couldn't for the life of him remember which ones they were. They handled so many different flowers every day at the shop that he had forgotten."

Everyone sitting around in the circle listened intently. Falman continued.

"Soon, his wife stood at his bedside all night, from dusk till dawn, whispering in a low voice: 'You did not love me at all. You never loved me.' And the florist grew ill from lack of rest. Finally, on the day after he had given her every kind of flower in the shop, he went out to the front of the shop and picked the wildflowers growing there. The summer had been hot, and the flowers were all dry and withered, but these were the last flowers he had to give her. That night was the first night she smiled. 'You did remember,' she said. 'You loved me after all—and such healthy, vibrant blossoms. These will bring me good company on my lonely road to the afterlife.' She smiled at the florist and gave him many thanks, and then she disappeared. And the next day—"

Everyone gulped.

"—The next day, the florist was found cold in his bed. When the townspeople went to her grave, they found the wildflowers he had left there in full bloom, as though they had drained the very life from the florist."

A long silence followed Falman's story. A chill wind blew, and the light from the lamp shivered and quaked. The story had been worse than they expected.

"That's a scary story."

"Scary is right!"

"You know, even when you're scared, a scary story is still pretty scary . . ."

"No kidding."

It wasn't the most convincing ghost story in the world. How could anyone have known what the florist and his wife's ghost talked about alone at his bedside? But no one was in a state of mind to point out its obvious flaws. They had all hoped that a story might pass the time, but now they were frightened out of their minds.

"I want to go home," said Breda, but nobody moved—no one wanted to leave by himself. They had thought they were at the sticky bottom of fear, but now they found that they were digging a hole in the bottom and going even deeper. Just sitting there in the circle made them even more scared. As one, they all stood up in an attempt to break the spell. They grabbed on to one another's sleeves and slowly resumed their walk toward whatever lay beyond Warehouse 12. They had all worked on this base for quite a while, but something about the night wind and the fear in their minds made the familiar scene around them look like another world. It was as though they were wandering through a strange, foreign land, and it wearied them in mind, body, and spirit.

They passed by Warehouse 9, then Warehouse 10, then

Warehouse 11, pushing and pulling one another along, each walking as closely as possible to their reluctant leader.

"Ohh . . ." moaned Fuery, grabbing onto Roy's sleeve. He hadn't meant to say anything, but as they got closer to the last warehouse, the groan came unbidden from his lips.

Finally, they arrived at Warehouse 12.

"See? Nothing," said Havoc. Beyond Warehouse 12 was only open space, and then the three small, lettered warehouses, A, B, and C. "No Warehouse 13," he said pointing with his chin. "When it's dark and you're scared, that 'B' looks like a '13,' that's all."

Indeed, in the darkness they couldn't see anything clearly at all. Breda lifted the lantern until they could make out the 'B' of the middle warehouse.

"But what about the digging noises? The woman searching for her bones?"

"Yeah! The digging sounds . . . and the weeping! Are you saying those are lies?" whimpered Fuery, clinging to Roy.

"You almost sound as if you *want* there to be a ghost," said Roy, scowling.

"No, it's just . . ." began Fuery. None of them wanted to come this far and then just go home without being 100 percent certain there was nothing there. They all perked up their ears and listened. They held their breath, trying to make out the sounds of weeping or digging, but they heard nothing, only the faint whistle of the wind.

"I don't hear anything."

"Maybe she's not digging tonight?"

"Possibly, but if we've come this close and we still can't hear anything, maybe it was just the sound of the wind after all. Falman, Fuery, you heard the sounds from outside the warehouse complex, right? So you were on the other side of that wall. Noises can sound strange at a distance sometimes."

Roy's explanation did seem rather persuasive.

"True, it's no proof, but if you think about it, it was most likely a trick of the ears."

"I suppose," said Fuery, fighting the fear inside him. Then he lifted his eyes and looked at Roy. "I guess . . . if we can't find the source of the sound here, it's nowhere to be found. It was just a trick of the ears. It was the wind." Fuery had conquered his fears.

"Right. We all happy?" said Roy, turning around. Havoc, Breda, and Falman all smiled, nodding. "Right! Mission complete," said Roy, the relief in his voice apparent. He had no desire to have a paranormal encounter himself. While he had always doubted things like ghosts existed, the night air and the ghost story had gotten to him, too, and he was glad that it was over. In the end, there was nothing to worry about.

With the same kind of uplifting feeling one gets after completing a long journey, they all turned to go back the way they had come. The adventure was over. Just then, the moon peeked out from between a crack in the clouds. The area around them was bathed in cool, pale moonlight, and then—

"*Arrrgh!*"

"*Eeeek!*"

"*Nooo . . . !*"

They saw it: a pile of freshly turned earth, glistening with dew in the moonlight—right in the space between Warehouse 12 and the lettered warehouses. The black mound of dirt stood before them in the pale blue light, daring them to run screaming.

Havoc took a step back, and Fuery began to shake uncontrollably. Behind him, Falman's hand on the lantern and Breda's legs also began to quiver. The truth none of them hoped to find now stared them in the face. Roy, cursing his own quaking legs, began to walk toward the pile.

"No, don't go, Colonel!"

"What if the ghost attacks you?"

"L-let's come back here when it's light!"

The fear in the group had reached new heights, but Roy still walked forward. As commanding officer, he had to get to the bottom of this. He dragged the four behind him, still clinging to his arms. When they reached the edge of the dirt mound, they saw it. There, in a shallow pit by the mound, a white bone lay glinting in the light.

"I didn't think it would really be there," said Roy, in shock. He didn't want a ghost haunting his base, his home away from home. Bones, buried here! It was worse than any ghost story. Looking closer, he saw more bones, scattered in the dirt. It was all real. At the moment when his fear of the unknown became a horrifying reality, Roy felt another feeling: responsibility. He had to figure out whose bones lay here. For the others, especially the two who heard the sounds at night, it had only increased their fear.

"That sound, that sound . . ." repeated Fuery.

"It's really here."

"It's probably out there looking at us!"

They all looked around, fearfully. Every single one of them believed in ghosts at that moment. Roy gave them a stern look. "First things first. We're burying these bones."

A chorus of pleas rose up in response.

"If we touch the bones, she'll be mad!"

"She'll haunt us till our dying days!"

"Please, Colonel, it's too dangerous!"

Seeing his men all quaking in their boots, Roy stooped down and picked up a fallen branch. "Then fine, I'll do it myself. I don't know why it has to be me—you were the ones that got me out here in the first place."

The four of them grabbed onto his arm, trying to keep him from deepening the hole with his stick.

"No, please, sir! Don't they say to let sleeping bones lie?"

"If you anger the ghost, Colonel, she'll haunt us all!"

Roy growled. "What are you saying? I'm just going to

bury them until we have time to do a formal investigation. We can't just leave them lying out here."

"But the ghost collected all these herself! She'll get angry if we touch them!" pleaded Fuery.

"Colonel, what if a ghost comes to us every night, just 'cause we were here with you?" said Havoc and then added in a spooky voice, "What if she says, 'Why didn't you stop the colonel from touching my bones?!'"

"Eeek! That would be really scary!" wailed Fuery.

Roy tried to calm the panicked men. "If that happens, I'll take the fall for you. Just tell her I did it, okay?" But it wasn't enough to ease their fears.

"No way, Colonel, I know you—you'll tell her to go haunt us, not you!"

"Yeah, you'll just save yourself at our expense!"

"Fine," said Roy, "I hereby swear that I'll take all responsibility for this, supernatural or otherwise, okay?"

Havoc shook his head. "We can't go on just your word, Colonel."

"So what should I do?" said Roy, exasperated.

In the end, Havoc pulled out a scrap of paper out of his pocket, and on it, Roy wrote an oath swearing that if anything negative came out of this, he would assume full responsibility. Now they had something to show the ghost if she chose to haunt them. Something *official*. The four seemed to accept this, so they went about gathering sticks to help Roy dig. They had a large hole in a few minutes. They tenderly picked up the bones, laid them in the pit, and reburied them.

So ended the first Eastern Command Paranormal Investigation.

"Let's go home."

"Yeah."

They were all exhausted. Tossing down their sticks, they made their way back to the central hall.

"Let's bring some flowers out here tomorrow," suggested Havoc, walking next to Roy.

"Good idea," said Roy. The rest concurred.

"I wonder what flowers she likes," said Breda.

Everyone looked at the others. Even Breda stopped short. They all thought back to the story of the flower-seller's wife.

THE NEXT MORNING, the men disappeared behind the warehouses, each carrying as many flowers as he could. Hawkeye watched them suspiciously. "What's going on there?"

"Oh, nothing," said Roy, looking sheepish. They hadn't mentioned either the rumors or the late-night investigation to Hawkeye. Saying something would only get them chastised for running around like schoolboys at work. Then again, they *had* found something, so maybe it would be okay.

Regardless, Roy couldn't bring himself to talk about it. What they found last night had been such a surprise, he wouldn't even know where to begin. In the worst-case scenario, the military might have been involved in this. Maybe someone had been secretly killed, or there was a conspiracy of some sort.

Roy planned to bring his findings to his superior's attention later that day and request an investigation. Until everything was cleared up, he wanted to leave the ghost alone. "I'll tell you about it eventually," he told Hawkeye at last. Although there was little chance Hawkeye would accept such a brush-off, after a brief pause, she thankfully turned the conversation back to work matters.

Roy took some documents from Hawkeye and looked out the window. He could see the line of twelve warehouses, looking as they always did. Beyond that, the place where they had found the bones was buried in flowers. The total cost of the flowers had been more than 10,000 sens, but they thought that if that would calm the ghost even a little, it was a small price to pay.

At noon, the members from last night's mission ate together in the central courtyard. After having the rest of the night to calm down, they were all quite proud of themselves for being so courageous.

"It was pretty scary out there, but I'm glad we got to the bottom of it."

"We couldn't just let the rumors go on—that would have annoyed that ghost more than anything else, I bet."

"I think we did the right thing."

"You're right."

"Still, the colonel was the calmest of all of us. He did really good out there."

"Bah," said Roy, scowling.

"We all look up to you, you know," said Havoc, smiling innocently.

The group cracked up laughing. They wore the easy smiles of those who have seen the same hardship and come through it victorious. The ringing laughter caught the attention of Hawkeye's dog, who came bounding into their circle. Fuery cheered and greeted the pup with open arms while Breda shot up and ran as fast as he could to the other side of the yard. Everyone laughed again. It was a perfect, easygoing afternoon on base.

HAWKEYE CALLED OUT to them. "Did something happen? Why is everyone so cheery today?"

"No, no, it's nothing," said Roy. They all smiled. The dog wagged his tail enthusiastically, happy because they were happy. Then he raised his front paw and waved it in the air.

"What's wrong? You hungry?" said Fuery, holding the dog's paw and talking to him. The dog licked his face. "Hah hah, that tickles!"

"He wants his snack," said Hawkeye, going into her office and coming back with a bag. From the bag she pulled a big, juicy, T-bone steak.

Everyone's eyes shot to the steak. The bone looked horribly familiar.

"Y-you give him T-bone steaks?" said Roy, aghast.

"Yup! He loves them," said Hawkeye, holding the steak out to the dog. "Eat up, doggie! You're a growing boy! You need all the calcium you can get!"

The dog grabbed the steak out of her hand and spun around ecstatically in circles, then ran off down the path by the warehouses.

"Aw, he's gone off to hide it again." Hawkeye looked after the dog with fondness in her eyes. "Once he finishes the meat, he likes to race off and hide the bones. It's so adorable!"

Hawkeye smiled a rare warm smile, but no one was looking. Their eyes were all fixed on the dog, running past Warehouse 1 . . . 2 . . . 3 . . . When it reached the end of the path, the dog suddenly turned and disappeared behind Warehouse 12.

"Oh, no . . ."

"The bone . . ."

"Those bones . . . "

"Behind the warehouse . . ."

Hawkeye turned to them. "Oh, yes, he hides them there all the time."

"Why didn't anyone notice?"

212

The group was huddled in a stairwell near the emergency exit of the main hall where no one would overhear them.

"It was so dark . . . and there were so many of them. I mean, we're amateurs! How could we know the bones weren't human?" said Havoc.

In subsequent investigations, they'd found out that the weeping noises were from the dog. He had recognized Fuery's footsteps from the other side of the wall and had snuffled and whined for attention. The only reason the digging sounds came at night was because there were too many other normal noises during the daytime to hear them. Furthermore, it seemed that the reason the dog had howled that night was that he was afraid they would dig up his stash of bones. The truth was mortifying.

They were exhausted and red with chagrin.

"My hands . . ." whispered Breda. "I touched bones with dog slobber on them!"

"Oh, go wash them, silly," said Havoc.

Breda ran off, moaning. Moments later they heard a rush of water from an outdoor faucet.

Falman looked at the paper he had just finished typing. "Colonel, about this investigation request . . ."

"Get rid of that this instant," barked Roy.

M.Sgt. Fuery swallowed as Falman ripped up the paper. "Colonel, all those flowers . . ."

"Clean them up too!"

After everything that had happened last night, they couldn't believe this.

Havoc held up a crumpled piece of paper. "Uh, sir, I took the money for those flowers out of expenses . . ."

"Hide it!"

BUT THINGS DIDN'T GO quite as planned. A few days later, Hawkeye called M.Sgt. Fuery to her desk. "This expense for 10,000 sens, what was it for?"

Fuery gulped. "Umm . . ."

In an effort to avoid detection, Havoc had typed up the description of the expenses and passed it to Breda, who passed it to Falman, who passed it to Fuery. Fuery was to give the paper to Roy, and once he signed it and gave it to accounting, the matter would be settled. It was their terrible luck that just as Fuery had been standing up to bring the paper to Roy, Hawkeye happened by and saw him. She recognized the expense report and took it out of his hands as he stood frozen in place.

"I'm heading over to Roy's desk right now. I'll take this for you."

She glanced down at the paper and stopped. She looked back up at Fuery. It was an unusually large sum for a daily expense, and of course, she wanted an explanation. Fuery looked around at everyone else in the room for support. In return, they gave him tense little smiles and encouraging nods. Sitting at the biggest desk, Roy glared icicles at Fuery, ordering him with his eyes to not say a word.

"What's this?"

"Um . . ." If Hawkeye found out how they had used the money, their late-night mission would be revealed. Not only would they get chewed out, but they'd have to pay the 10,000 sens out of their own pockets. If he didn't try his hardest now, he'd be letting everyone down, and the thought of Col. Mustang being mad at him was scary indeed.

At the same time, he knew Hawkeye would never fall for a lie. In his heart, Fuery weighed which was worse: Roy's anger or Hawkeye's wrath. He looked up into Hawkeye's clear brown eyes, staring back at him. It would be impossible to hide anything from her.

I'm sorry, he said to Roy silently, and then he began to speak, and the truth was out.

DAYS PASSED. Of course, the expense report was rejected. A dispute arose between the four enlisted men who wanted the guy with the biggest salary to pay. Roy thought they should split the cost evenly. He couldn't understand why he had to pay at all, since they had been the ones who dragged him into their scheme in the first place. M.Sgt. Fuery aside, the other three weren't rich, but they weren't exactly struggling either. Still, they liked having the cash for a night out every now and then. They wanted Roy at least to wait until their next raise. Neither side would budge, and so the stalemate dragged on.

Eventually, Roy lost. Havoc brought up that Roy had offered to take responsibility for "anything negative" that came out of their fact-finding mission, be it supernatural or otherwise—he even had written proof—and Roy had to pay.

"This is just a loan, you guys," muttered Roy. "You'd better pay up your shares when you get the money."

"Can I pay mine in ten installments?" asked Breda.

"Make it five."

"I'll pay you next payday," said Falman.

"You'd better."

"Can I wait until the payday after that?" asked Havoc. "There's something I want to buy next payday."

Roy sighed. "You're the least trustworthy of the lot, Havoc! Why should I give you an extension?"

Havoc grinned and shrugged.

To this day, Roy hasn't gotten any of his money back.

Afterword

HELLO. This is Makoto Inoue.

I really love *Fullmetal Alchemist*, so naturally, being allowed to write this novel made me very happy.

In order to completely immerse myself in the world of *Fullmetal Alchemist*, I spent many stressful days using my brain to its full capacity. But on the other hand, it was also enjoyable because I was able to spend time thinking about my favorite characters. It might have seemed like I was just sitting there zoning out, but inside my head I was adventuring in the *Fullmetal Alchemist* world with a backpack. Or, it might have seemed like I was clutching my head in worry, but inside my head Col. Mustang and 2nd Lt. Havoc were doing a comedy routine. After spending my days like this, I realized that I'd become even more of a fan than I was before.

To me, this *Fullmetal Alchemist* novel was a short visit into Hiromu Arakawa's world. I would be extremely happy if the readers, and of course Arakawa-sensei, can even get a small amount of enjoyment out of the book. (But I do apologize if you don't like it.)

As always, I received a great deal of support from many people on this project. First of all, I'd like to thank Arakawa-sensei, for taking time out of her busy schedule and teaching so many things about the *Fullmetal* world. I promised you that if I ever saw you at Toys"R"Us staring in rapture at Darth Vader that I would pretend not to know you, so if you see me rummaging for Gundam model kits, please just look the other way (heh).

I'd also like to thank my editor, Nomoto-san. She helped me out tremendously by giving me advice and replying very quickly to all of my questions. Also, during the planning stages she would tell me things like "*BOOM!* Bring this over here . . . and then *BLAM!* Put this down here . . ." or "*BAM!* Just like that!" and "Copy the whole thing—*WHOOSH!*— right now . . ." I really enjoyed hearing her using so many sound effects in actual conversations. And I'll never forget what she said that one time . . .

MAKOTO INOUE: (talking about the schedule for the end of the year) "Wow, Nomoto-san, it looks like you're going to be even busier than before."

NOMOTO-SAN: "No, no it's all just a part of my job! To me being busy is nothing but a bunch of . . . *HANNACHARA-BOO!*"

She would say all of this in her characteristically pleasant voice. She knew how to keep things fun even when the work became stressful. Three seconds later, I would be laughing so hard that my stomach hurt. Thank you, Nomoto-san.

Finally, I would like to sincerely thank all of the people who read this book. Thank you very much!

—MAKOTO INOUE

AFTERWORD?

HELLO, I'M JUST THE PERSON WHO DREW THE ILLUSTRATIONS. I'M NOT VERY GOOD AT WRITING AFTERWORDS SO I'VE DECIDED TO SEE WHETHER I CAN GET AWAY WITH DOING SOME MORE ILLUSTRATIONS WITH A THEME. I WANT TO THANK ALL THE FOLKS AT THE PUBLISHER'S OFFICE AND ALL OF THE READERS. THANK YOU VERY MUCH! I ALSO WANT TO THANK ALL OF THE EDITORS AS WELL.

2003.1 Hiromu Arakawa

OLDER BROTHER
RUSSELL TRINGAM

HIS SILVER EYES PEER OUT FROM BENEATH
BLOND HAIR THAT HAS BEEN CUT TO A
MODERATE LENGTH. HIS LIKEABLE PERSONALITY
AND SLIM BUILD GIVE HIM AN AIR OF MATURITY
THAT MAKES IT HARD TO BELIEVE THAT
HE IS THE SAME AGE AS EDWARD (OR IS HE?).

YOUNGER BROTHER
FLETCHER TRINGAM

HE HAS THE SAME BLOND HAIR AND
SILVER EYES AS HIS OLDER BROTHER,
BUT HIS SMALL BUILD AND TENDENCY
TO LOOK DOWNWARD GIVE HIM AN
AIR OF UNCERTAINTY. BUT HE IS
FIERCELY LOYAL TO HIS BROTHER
AND HAS A GENTLE HEART.